Hurt Hands That Healed

Hurt Hands That Healed

A Story of Violation and Redemption

Andrea Skeeter

RESOURCE *Publications* · Eugene, Oregon

HURT HANDS THAT HEALED
A Story of Violation and Redemption

Resource Publications
An Imprint of Wipf and Stock Publishers
199 W. 8th Ave., Suite 3
Eugene, OR 97401

www.wipfandstock.com

PAPERBACK ISBN: 978-1-6667-7833-5
HARDCOVER ISBN: 978-1-6667-7834-2
EBOOK ISBN: 978-1-6667-7835-9

VERSION NUMBER 01/03/24

All scripture quotations, unless otherwise indicated, are taken from the Holy Bible, Revised Standard Version, 1952.

Dedicated to the angels Angela & Karen that watched over me in the land of the living.

Contents

Preface

This is my story of me. I am me, and only I can tell my story. My earliest memories are painful at best, in body, mind, and spirit. The pages that follow describe those memories. The pain that these memories bear is due in large part to my family, yet also in no small part due to this fallen body of mine that still today remains fragile flesh and bones.

Life has presented me with many opportunities to travel and see this vast globe. I have met people from literally all over the world. My list of friends contains the names and stories of people from Antarctica to Russia, from North America to Australia. Learning to live my life to its fullest has given me some long nights and some tear-filled days. The journey has not been easy. My story is unlike any other and yet like so many others.

I hope and pray that the deep personal aspects of my life that I share with you will bless you and encourage you to trust the one God.

If only one of you finds hope for your future from having read about my past, then the words in this book will have accomplished my mission of sharing the living Christ as I have experienced him in my life. For I came to know him after having lived a tumultuous life apart from conscious awareness of him.

While we are not promised perpetual bouquets of roses and songs of love, life is worth living for what Christ does for us. He works at times without our seeing him and at other times with his being as clear to us as the light of the sun is bright to our eyes. No life is lived without trial, heartache, and pain. Sometimes the bad days outweigh the good ones, and moments of joy and happiness rendezvous with the grief and misery that lurk around the corner.

What are we to do? We are to live and love as if each day is our last and as if it is also our first. We forgive quickly and often because Christ has forgiven quickly and often—easier though it is to say than to live. Each morning sunrise and evening sunset, as well as the storminess in-between, provide us with an opportunity to experience joy in spite of sorrow, hope in spite of despair, and change in spite of inertia, all because Christ remains with us along the way.

Although my story was conceived and born of darkness, hatred, and death, the awesome God who created the universe looked out upon his creation and decided that he needed me to be in it nonetheless. The life I have lived in but a short length of time has felt in some instances like a soap opera and at other times like a horror film. And yet, as the only story that I can tell as my own, it is also my testimony to rejoice in the goodness of the Lord in the land of the living.

Andrea Skeeter

1

Young Me

Two fledgling teenagers, soul-tied and body-bound for what seemed like the time it would take lightening to flash across the sky, gave birth to far more than either of them could imagine. In the passion of the moment, destined to shed more than a few tears of joy and sorrow for some time to come, they produced the fruit of their wedlock, the divine fortune of their union—me.

He ran for the prize in track and field at his high school. Five miles away, down a few winding roads, she took to the field as a cheerleader and majorette at a rival school across town. As their paths crossed at the occasional football game or track meet, they greeted one another with a brief glance and a smile.

Being the older and a grade ahead of him, and living at home with her parents and three siblings, she enjoyed the privileges of an active senior year. He, the younger in this relationship and a grade behind her, lived under the same roof with his father and three of his seven brothers. Both desired the opportunity to live in liberty apart from their respective families and both were willing to work for this freedom.

Popularity with the opposite sex met no barrier. Despite pre-existing relationships that complicated their introduction—in his case, another woman—her bright smile and cheery personality, coupled with her physical agility, entangled his affections at first glance.

She, too, was intrigued. As with many a woman in passing, his cold-black, shiny, loosely-curled hair and cappuccino-tone skin honeyed her eyes instantly in his direction.

So it happened. His hawk eyes, like a laser beam, zeroed in.

On the playing field sideline, beneath the bright stadium lights glaring against the Friday night sky, he spots her in her majorette uniform, twirling her baton. The fact that as a senior she is about to graduate doesn't matter to him at all, nor does the hurt he will cause the woman he lets go.

After the game, he musters the courage and asks her for a date, and a flash beginning becomes prelude to a long ending.

* * *

Their dating remained casual for the rest of his time in high school. Once she received her diploma, she attended classes on a historically black college and university campus in a nearby city. For a short while she continued to live at home and commute to school. During this time he internalized the meaning of hard work before finishing high school. He committed himself fully to working for a company before being considered an adult. After he finished high school the following year, they moved into an apartment together. He continued in the role he had obtained through a local vocational-technical school, and kept this job for another forty-plus years.

Living life on their own presented them with new challenges that they were not prepared to tackle or overcome. Many conflicts arose throughout their relationship, but they were determined to make it work. As they grew closer to one another, a dark secret was building behind the scenes. Soon they would marry and move to a new city. During this time he was having a house built for her. It was almost as if he was trying to buy her forgiveness for the time some day when he would need it.

This young marriage was froth with troubles. The very concept of marriage, two becoming one, inherently means that both individuals will have to change to "fit" together as one unit. Like most young marriages a lack of communication and unmet expectations caused them to begin to resent one another. She was used to being a fiercely independent woman like her own mother, and he was raised by a widowed father that had not fully equipped him on how to be a husband. Naturally, arguing and miscommunicating their needs and desires with one another became second nature in their daily interactions. This marriage, built on shaky ground without a solid foundation or insulating walls of comfort, would be continuously tested.

Together they thought a baby would make the situation better, and my sister was born. Eighteen months later, I would enter this family in distress.

2

The Courthouse

Childhood memories for many if not all adults bring to mind those sweet and loving hugs and kisses they received from their parents. But earliest memories of my mother and father are as far from sweet and loving as the east is from the west.

I can see my father and mother standing before the doors of the old brick and mortar courthouse, not fighting for the rights of others but fighting each other. I don't mean physically fighting, I mean wounding and damaging each other's hearts to the breaking point.

Yet my memories of such occasions are not all bad. Or at least not of those moments before we left for the courthouse, when my mother woke up my sister and me early in the morning to get my sister ready for school while I played with my toys.

Dressing us up was her way of daily creating her own little Black porcelain dolls to be admired. She had already picked out my clothes and placed them neatly on the brown floral coach in the living room, along with a pair of white ruffled socks and my black patent leather shoes.

Sundays were the same. As we prepared for church, she was determined that we would look stylish and girlie the moment we set foot out the door. For just that, she brought forth the bucket

containing hundreds if not thousands of creatively designed bar-
rettes. Any shape, color, size, and you name it, we had it. It was
imperative that we look our best since it was true that how we appeared to others was how this woman we called Momma judged
herself. Little did I know at that time, as small as I was, that dressing us up would remain her sole preoccupation when it came to
parenting. For with times to come and memories never to be forgotten, she unmercifully dressed us down with her words.

* * *

After sitting for moments that seemed like months to a three-
year-old, what with my hair being brushed, combed, pulled,
twisted, and tamed, I was ready to be done with getting dressed.
I wanted to get going.

I distinctly remember the day. We were parked in front of the
courthouse. I was wearing a mint-green sweat suit with a poodle
sewn on the front that was covered with soft white puffs begging
to be pulled. My ruffled socks had slid down into those shiny black
patent leather shoes with a strap across the ankle and a bow tied
to the toe, looking all bright and new right out of the box. Strangers about town commented on how cute I was. Just as I had been
taught, I politely responded, "Thank you!"

After stepping out of the car at the county courthouse set way
back in the woods miles from the locally owned grocery store we
had just left behind, I spotted him.

I seldom saw him, but whenever I did, my momma always
said "that's him" as she referred to my daddy. At this point in my
life he was no more than a stranger. Not as in "stranger danger"
but as a stranger simply because of not knowing much about him.
Apart from his title and the old brick and mortar courthouse to
which I had affixed my first memories of "him," I didn't know
who he was.

* * *

So, having approached the courthouse door, there I stood catching a glimpse of him in a moment of delicate exchange, as a smile broke out across his face, when suddenly my momma's hand grabbed hold of me and snatched me away lest I continue to stare at him too long.

She handed me over to the play area attendant whose job it was to safeguard me from the agony taking place down the hall in the courtroom: *Disputing facts. Making allegations. Demeaning one another's character. Showing no regard whatsoever for the love once shared between two ex-lovers.*

In the play area I could build things with wooden blocks, race the toy cars, and relish the pictures in Dr. Seuss books lining the shelves—all distractions to offer me solace outside of the war zone inside.

Those courthouse visits went on for years, well into my longing childhood. And then one day my momma announced that the case was settled and closed. The divorce was final.

But instead of a divorcee decree, the judge should have pronounced a declaration of war. For what followed was nothing shy of me diving repeatedly into the trenches of battle as the bombs of matrimonial warfare exploded all around me and the shrapnel of bitterness flew in every direction, ripping out my heart.

3

Birthday

My teacher had just called out my name, exclaiming "Happy birthday!" as she announced the class birthdays for the month. When asked for the very first time, "How old are you?" I answered by raising both hands high in the air, extending five fingers with one hand and a single finger with the other—totaling six altogether.

Could anyone present that day have imagined just how important that moment was for me? For until I turned six, my birthdays had been anything but special. Every prior year's birthday cake contained multiple names—my cousins' mixed in with mine—written across the top of the icing. And "Happy Birthday" was sung to all of us all at once. But now, finally, the day had come when I didn't have to share my birthday with anyone else.

So, there I sat fidgeting in my seat with excitement, when out of the blue I heard the principal making announcements over the loudspeaker.

"Happy birthday, Andrea Skeeter!" he said.

My teacher and classmates erupted in thunderous applause and shouting.

* * *

Early that morning at sunrise, I had awakened with visions of a yummy birthday cake, ice cream, balloons, singing, and dancing, all rolled into one. Leaping out of the bed that I shared with my mother and sister, the second I opened my eyes they each exclaimed, one after the other, "Happy birthday!"

Joy welled up inside me like the glistening sun rising over the ocean, covering my half-forgotten worries with its rays of warmth.

My mother picked out a cute dress for me to wear. She combed my hair and tied beautiful bows in it, the kind reserved for church on Sundays. This was going to be by far the best birthday I had ever had. I wasn't about to miss it. I thought that whatever happened when I returned home from school, it would be even better than all the ice cream and cake I could eat.

Yet, contrary to the early dawn's expectations and visions, a celebration with rose petals, streamers, jelly beans, and lollipops was simply not meant to be.

* * *

At that time, my parents were still going through their divorce, which was also a divorce from us, their children. To say the least, their relationship remained fervently hostile.

Officers on the local police force knew them quite well from the times my mother had called for help when my father returned us home ten to twenty minutes late from our weekend visits with him.

While my father often bore the brunt of my mother's bitterness, anger, and aggression, little did I know that she had a never-ending well from which to draw and spew her venom upon others, and especially upon me.

After the school day had ended, I boarded the bus and headed to my babysitter's apartment which served as a second home for me. Many life-changing events were to take place there over the course of time.

My sister and I affectionately called our sitter "Aunt P." She and her two daughters, one a newborn and the other three years older than I, shared their space with us as if we were family. The older daughter eventually helped to shape my timid personality into a more demonstrative one. Her little baby sister, whose lovely chocolate skin, graced with coal-black curls atop her head, with the whites of her eyes shining like a full moon against the midnight sky, became like a little sister to me as well—a fun toy to play with, and one who didn't hesitate to play back.

Having gotten off the bus I headed upstairs to the apartment where I heard voices murmuring, some more familiar than others. Upon entering, I saw my father across the room. His girlfriend, sitting near the door, grabbed hold of my face, kissed me, and said, "Happy birthday, little girl!"

As others called out "happy birthday" to me, a joyful feeling overwhelmed me and I began to cry. Perhaps the tears were due to the excitement bubbling up within me as the center of attention as I walked about hugging all the people who lavished me with their "happy birthdays." Or perhaps the tears were due to something less obvious at first glance, something like a missing candle on a birthday cake lit with five candles when it should have been lit with six.

She was at work at the time. While I didn't consciously miss her so long as the attention was focused on me, I believe my tears were speaking words that I could neither fully entertain nor so much as form on my lips. For as I scanned the room, even though that one important person was distinctly absent from the party, the adults were actually talking with one another and not just yelling and screaming and hurling obscenities like the ones I heard at home.

After hugging my father, he told me that he wanted to take me to the store so that I could choose whatever toy I wanted for my birthday. My face blossomed with elation as if I had just won mega-millions in the lottery even though I was barely acquainted with that outlandish, wishful sort of adult thinking that invariably crashed into the rocks of reality. Wishful childhood thinking alone was enough for me to yelp "Yes!" in response to his invitation.

But now, it was time for the birthday cake.

I don't remember just what it looked like, and I can't recall its flavor or whatever cartoon character stood atop its swirls of icing. But I do remember that after we cut and ate the cake, my daddy led me to his car so we could head over to the toy store to buy my present. In my eager state of mind I was already thinking that we'd be coming back to the apartment with the entire toy store hitched to the back of the car.

As we strolled inside the store from aisle to aisle, my eyes lit up at the sight of every conceivable toy I had ever dreamed of owning. Repeatedly, I said, "I want this one, Daddy! I want that one!"

My father, on the other hand, countered each of my requests by saying that I could have only one toy. This quickly deflated my wishful thinking like air swishing out of a punctured balloon. Nevertheless, my determination persisted. I picked up yet another toy and handed it to him. In a few more steps, spying still another and another, I handed him the next just as soon as he put down the latter. And so on we went, up one aisle and down the other.

At last, being visibly annoyed with my indecisiveness, he told me to stop. In his most adamant tone of voice he said that I must choose one toy, and one toy only, so that he could pay for it and we could leave because he needed to go to work.

Hesitating, I considered my choices and finally selected a doll. There was nothing especially memorable about it except that she was my doll and my birthday gift. While I hadn't won the lottery, I had gained something much more important.

I had claimed something that was just mine and nobody else's.

* * *

When the clock struck midnight and my birthday officially ended, I felt the entire day's enjoyment rushing through my body. As she came through the door to pick me up, I wanted my mother to admire my doll just as much as I. I wanted her to share my happiness and joy.

"My daddy took me to the store and let me buy this doll!" I exclaimed.

With that, the smile with which she entered the apartment turned upside down into a frightful frown. Fiery fury exploded from her lips and instantly consumed my happiness.

Yelling profanities at my sitter, she ordered us, "Go to the car!"

As my sister and I hurried toward the door, she spat more of her venom at the sitter.

"Don't you ever let that man take my children without my permission! I will call the cops on him and you!"

Simply put, my birthday was over. But the night was not done with me.

After the car door slammed shut behind us, my mother entered the driver's seat and for the first time that night slapped me across the face while repeating the same injunction she had hurled at Aunt P.—"Don't go anywhere with your father without my permission!"

My recollection of all that had happened that day raced through my mind as I wondered what I'd done so terribly wrong to deserve her wrath. My joy and laughter had totally collapsed beneath her rage, like a rag doll drenched in the rain.

The ride home did little except further fan the flames of fire fuming inside her. Finally, when she seemed at last to calm down, she asked me what I'd gotten from the store.

Quivering, I held out my doll for her to admire.

Then she did the unthinkable. She rolled down the window and flung my doll, along with all of my happy birthday memories, out of the car.

* * *

Arriving home, still visibly agitated, she walked into the house and demanded, "Bring me my belt!"

As I moved slowly down the hallway and opened the door to her bedroom and touched the wall to feel for the light switch, all I could do was wonder what awful crime I had committed to warrant the dreaded belt. In times past, my disobedience and stubbornness had received a well-deserved punishment. But her deliberate act of injustice went far beyond the penal law that governed our house.

I was all too familiar with the belt. It had been applied to me many times when I knew I was at fault. But this crime, whatever it was, was not my fault. I had done exactly as my father had told me when he said, "Let's go and get you your birthday present." This time I was being punished for my obedience.

As I returned to the living room with the belt in my hand, my mother sat waiting on the couch. She instructed my sister to go to bed. This was to be a private moment between the two of us, though anything but loving and affectionate.

For now I felt as much rage and hatred toward her as she had directed at me.

4

Stand Up for Yourself

A benefit of being born the second child is having someone else to look up to and admire, as well as be a constant playmate.

My older sister was born seventeen months before me, which prompted my mother to dress us often in identical attire. Strangers regularly asked, "Are they twins?" which on most occasions infuriated one or both of us. Although close in age, our facial features were unmistakably distinct.

Imagine the Energizer bunny cast as my sister's body. She kept going and going and going from the time we awakened until we fell asleep at night. In search for a single toy, she destroyed our freshly cleaned bedroom in less than two minutes. She ran back and forth down our long hallway for hours at a time. I often sat on the floor observing her unending energy propel her into constant motion.

Physicians diagnosed her as having ADHD (attention deficit hyperactivity disorder). At the time, I didn't know the meaning of that acronym, but I could see its symptoms exhibited in her largely uncontrollable restiveness, fidgeting, and breaking things. Lacking the ability to contain her physical impulses, she indulged in acrobatic feats without regard to repercussions as she swung from doors and jumped off the back of the couch, incurring minor injuries when she landed on the floor. Between the ages of two and ten her stunts caused my mother constant frustration and worry.

Around the age of five, I developed my own method of dealing with my sister's hyperactive behavior. I first offered her the verbal warning, "I don't want to play anymore." When that didn't work I gently tapped her arm or leg. Finally, as a last resort, I gave a resounding pop to the center of her back with the palm of my hand, which made her fold like a lawn chair. Little was my remorse when she failed to heed my several warnings.

My mother, on the other hand, took a dim view of my swift action and reprimanded me with a spanking, saying, "You're going to hurt that girl," as if that had been my intention, which it wasn't.

This was our daily sibling routine until a different girl emerged in me, one that was much more willing to fight fairly.

* * *

When I started going to a new babysitter's house and was introduced to her two daughters, I instantly sensed that I would never be quite the same. Her elder daughter was the oldest among us four, the youngest being a newly born living doll as cute as a button. Together we formed a family of "cousins."

During the day, while we older ones were in school, the baby remained at home with her mother in a quiet and peaceful atmosphere where she could hear her own voice and enjoy independent play. But once our yellow school bus rolled down the street and its doors flung open, the peace and quiet was all over. Each of us older three fought one another for the opportunity to hold and attend to the youngest.

Our town, which was quaint and intimate, held deep roots for us all. It was impossible to walk into a store and not hear "You belong to so and so" when someone called the name of one my relatives. The family resemblances were easy to spot in our noses, cheeks, and facial structures. More often than not, those relational connections were correctly identified. Sometimes a person would call out the name of my grandfather Shephard or my great aunt or my uncles. But often I heard my mother's name mentioned when someone recognized her features in mine.

Once, years later, when looking through some old photographs, I picked up a picture and told my mother that I didn't recall posing for it. She laughed and explained, "You wouldn't remember because it's not you, it's me." As I stared at the bright-eyed, chocolate-drop baby with skin and curly hair just like my own, it was as if I were looking in the mirror at myself.

* * *

The babysitter's elder daughter brought a different dynamic into the family. She and her little sister shared the same mother but had different fathers. This likely accounted for the stark contrast in their personalities. Or maybe their differences were due to the Creator's uniquely made design.

The intersection of my life with that of the infant daughter changed me considerably. Our interactions began with her commanding, "Bring me this" or "Give me that." I readily complied. And why so? Because I despised conflict.

I avoided quarrels and altercations whenever possible. The shouting and yelling that I had witnessed between my parents had left a stain upon my world and a bitter taste in my mouth. After having observed my sister fail to follow parental directions, it seemed better that I be a person who complied.

Just so, each afternoon we each received our own snack. I held mine for a little while before eating it, even as others tore into theirs and guzzled them down. I remember an occasion when my sister hurriedly finished hers and then glanced over at mine. "Yes, you can have one," I said to her, as she asked for one of the two cakes packaged together. Deferential though I was, my cousin, upon observing the transaction, took it like the last straw that broke the camel's back. She jumped from her seat and yelled, "No, she cannot have yours!"

What was wrong with my sharing? I wondered. As I opened the package to hand the cake to my sister, before I knew it my cousin lunged and hit me.

"Tell her no!" she demanded.

Speaking through the tears rolling down my face, I said it was okay that I wanted to share, which made her all the more enraged.

"Those are yours. Don't give her what's yours!" she insisted. Then she proceeded to hit my sister and told her to leave me alone.

Saddened, and hunched over with her head hung low, my sister went outside to play.

I did not realize it at the time, but this was the first encounter of many that trained me for the battles that lay ahead. Within months I gained my assertiveness, speaking less through words and more through actions.

As we sat on the living room floor one day, I held in my hands a toy that my cousin said she wanted. I firmly responded, "No!"

My cousin immediately threw a punch landing on my arm. I swung back and hit her. She then retaliated by grabbing my ponytail to lift me from where I sat as I took another swing at her torso. We slapped, punched, and scratched each other, tussling back and forth until eventually, because she was bigger and older and stronger than I, she seized the toy.

But my surrender was not without a fight. I punched with fists, not words.

* * *

Girls my age generally learned that they should discuss their conflicts until all parties reached an agreement. By contrast, my cousins taught me the art of the physical fight waged with very few words. Thereby, I thought, I could settle disputes once and for all in my favor.

As I grew older, recalling those lessons, I engaged in numerous physical altercations. Whenever other females argued with me, I quickly ended the stalemate with a violent outburst. In elementary and middle school I enjoyed being an instigator to demonstrate my newly found social skills. Yet since physical fighting created more problems than it offered solutions, in time I learned to employ hand-to-hand combat as a last resort rather than a first.

Before I had become so outwardly demonstrative, I had been a quiet, timid soul whom most people overlooked as I tucked myself within, withholding my opinions from the surrounding chatter. For the sake of feeling secure, I guarded my words like precious stones. Only on special occasions, or when I felt entirely comfortable in someone's presence, did I outwardly display them.

Yet during this transformative year and a half at my new sitter's house, I turned those word-stones into heated bullets that could destroy virtually anyone who stood in my path. With the turn of a few choice phrases, I could make another person feel like the dirt beneath my shoes.

The saying, "sticks and stones may break my bones, but words will never hurt me," did not apply. Words were power and I enjoyed feeling powerful. It would take a monumental failure to awaken me to the reality that words could change me as well.

5

Violated

I had changed babysitters frequently by the time I entered the second grade. Most of them had tolerated my mother's child-drearing ideas only briefly. As the first day of school approached, I was overcome with nervous tension.

What will happen this year? What field trips will we go on? Who will be my classmates? Such questions filled my mind the night before school started. Newfound confidence in my fighting ability did not keep my anxious emotions at bay. As it was, events at school caused only half of my troubled thoughts. For I was once again to go to the house of a new sitter with no young children of her own. Besides caring for my sister and me, she tutored other children.

The sitter resided in a familiar neighborhood that held fond memories for me. The buildings themselves were of no particular significance apart from the people I mentally associated with them, one of whom was my great aunt who lived in the same apartment complex a few buildings away. Everyone knew her by name, and I, for one, had spent a great deal of time in her home.

When entering my great aunt's house, the first things one noticed decorating the walls were pictures of my sister and me as infants. The apartment was quaint like the town. A straight line of sight extended from the front door all the way through to the back bedroom window. The kitchen had just enough space for two people to stand and turn around. Situated next to a low table, the living room couch faced a love seat with a walkway in between. Each of the two bedrooms contained a bed, a dresser, and only a foot's width of floor for walking from one side to the other.

My great aunt and I had a lot in common. She stood tall like an ebony tree, grand and statuesque. Endowed with curves from her lips to her hips, men took instant notice of her whenever she entered the room. I had the good fortune of having inherited her body shape.

With a gentle yet firm hand she expressed her love for us. Earlier in my life, I had spent so many days in her apartment that I began to call her "Momma," which infuriated my mother so that she stopped dropping us off there to stay, allowing us instead only the occasional brief visit.

My great aunt had a special relationship with my grandfather who was her brother. As the oldest child, she quit school in the third grade to help take care of him and the rest of her younger siblings. Her bond with my grandfather was unmistakably exuberant as they exchanged both laughter and curses with one another. He adored her, so much so that he named his second child after her.

A strong, towering Black man, my grandfather strolled daily down the sidewalk to visit his big sister. He wore khaki pants, a white t-shirt, and blue suspenders. He jingled coins in his pocket as he marched toward her door carrying a brown paper bag containing a six-pack of beer and a pack of cigarettes for his indulgence throughout the day. The coins were intended for his granddaughters.

Just so, he met us on the porch and handed each of us coins for buying candy from the ice cream truck that beckoned our attention with its sweet-sounding song calling all the children in the neighborhood to come running with their money. The three of us—my cousin, my sister, and I—felt like millionaires as we got in line to make our tasty purchases. We each returned home with a bag of sweets costing a penny apiece.

Such were the carefree moments of innocence that this kid with a candied smile on her face wished to last her a lifetime.

* * *

My sitter's sixteen-year-old nephew offered to help me with my homework. At first he did so by assisting me with difficult assignments.

The school had a policy of awarding pizza coupons to the students who read books at home for a certain number of days each month. The thought of pizza was a powerful incentive, so I read outside of school as much as possible. To that end, and to be certain that I received my reward, my aunt's nephew volunteered his aid with my reading log. His kindness, so it seemed, warranted my trust.

Moreover, my mother had inspected the house before allowing me to spend countless nights there. And in keeping with parental due diligence, she had asked questions about who would be in the house with my sister and me each day after school. Assuredly, then, it was safe place to be.

"Come, I have something in the room I want to show you," the nephew said to me one afternoon.

With that simple invitation he led me down the hallway into the bedroom and motioned for me to sit next to him on the bed. With apprehension I complied.

As he unzipped his pants, I wondered what he was hiding inside. He then lifted my right hand and placed it within.

Feeling anxious, my immediate impulse was to stop. But he squeezed my fingers against whatever was hidden. And as I sought to yank my hand away, he held an even tighter grip over my fingers, whispering, "It's okay to squeeze harder." So I did.

Despite my not knowing precisely what was hidden out of sight, the encounter felt far less like a pleasant surprise than a serious violation. In a room with one window across from the door, the closet open next to the entrance, and a floral comforter on the bed that was of no comfort at all, a few minutes seemed like hours.

"This will be our little secret," he said.

And with that, the innocence of a little girl with the candied smile on her face shattered forever.

* * *

We lived deep in the countryside surrounded by massive trees and endless fields producing crops for seasonal harvest. Three gallant pine trees shaded our yard, providing ample space for us children to play.

In the summer months, ticks awaited in the grass, ready to attach themselves to our tender flesh as we rolled on the ground. Daily, and forcibly with tweezers, either my mother or an aunt plucked a tick from at least one of us, carefully grabbing the tick's head lest it remain embedded, and striking a match to sear it in the flame.

The nightly ritual involved a physical inspection occasionally followed by an inquiry into the overall state of our bodily affairs. My mother sometimes asked questions like, "Did you break this?" or "Did you eat that?" presuming the answer she already knew. But then at times, when we were stepping out of the bathtub or getting ourselves dressed, she posed a question that begged an answer to alleviate her lingering uncertainty.

"Has anyone touched you or hurt you in your private parts?"

I did not know how to answer the question. For whenever I shared hurtful things with her, I was bound to experience heartache. If I could not trust my mother with something as valuable as my birthday doll, then how could I trust her with something far more personal? Consequently, I answered with a quiet and insincere "No."

* * *

I walked into my sitter's house afraid each afternoon, not knowing whether or not he would be there. It was not his presence that troubled me so much as did his heart's secret desire. I lived through unimaginable horror in that apartment, in that room, and in my mind, with every imposition of his body.

Each day, successively, he pursued the fulfillment of his devious appetite until finally he had intercourse with me and I became thoroughly defiled.

Each thrust of his pelvis into my tiny frame tore a hole into my spirit. His heavy breathing atop me sucked the breath from my lungs as my legs fought not to give way to the pressure.

I cried every day and night. I hid my tears where no one could see them, and my screams where no one could hear them.

I suffered in silence. In a world of six billion people, I dwelt alone, abandoned.

The first day of intercourse, his invitation excited me. But with each subsequent invasion, I cried and died yet another death within. I had initially arrived at the door of that house innocent and naïve, sheltered from the darkest darkness of the world, and from the guile of that sinful person. What had I done to deserve such torture? And what was I to do to protect myself from the primeval urges of a teenage boy who knew nothing whatsoever about becoming a man?

As the days turned into weeks, and the weeks into months, I wondered if his brutish torment would ever end.

I pondered those questions for years with the pain of sexual trauma as my endless reality, in the hope that some day I might find my way to change the unchangeable.

* * *

My interactions with my father were limited and infrequent. Every other weekend, alternate holidays, and one week of the summer were deemed sufficient, according to the court, for a daughter to receive the love and protection of her father.

For me there was no luxury of midweek phone calls, nor did he attend my school events and field trips. Only later did I learn that the reason for his inconsistent, neglectful fathering was due to his own misguidance as a result of which he miserably failed me.

The entire ordeal: an abusive mother, an irresponsibly inattentive father, and a perversely virile sixteen-year-old boy, altered my life's trajectory beyond anything an eight-year-old girl could possibly imagine.

I viewed the whole world as a hateful and hate-filled place. I could not trust anyone, least of all those who were supposed to safeguard my life. I saw everything and everyone through shaded dark glasses.

If only I could just keep on living, perhaps someday I would stumble upon a blessing and with it be blessed.

6

My End Is Near

With each passing day's infringement upon my fragile spirit and tainted body, the prevailing darkness continued to creep over me and blind the light that once shined in my eyes. It became difficult for me to look in the mirror. The little girl glancing back at me was decaying from the inside out.

Life at home at no point had been easy. With a mother who refused to show love and affection to her very offspring, plus a family friend determined to inflict his unbridled sexual appetite upon a small child, how could I not have been thrown into a state of perpetual perplexity and relentless shame?

My life didn't reflect the idyllic Disney movies that had captivated my attention, nor did it provide the happy endings of so many of the books I had read. Life, for me, felt more like the aftermath of death wreaking its daily putridness upon my soul.

Night after night dark objects with razor-sharp edges morphing into the cylindrical shapes of teeth encroached upon my restless sleep, devouring more and more of my spirit. By the time I was due to awake, thousands of teeth rotated clockwise and then counterclockwise, dripping blood that slowly drowned out the light.

What was I to do? I could not close my eyes without seeing those painful images, each representing a hurtful place or time in my life, or, as the rapper, singer, songwriter, Lauryn Hill, put it, "Killing Me Softly."

* * *

I was no more than three or four years old when I first took up crayons for coloring pictures. The crayon had great power to release my budding creativity. But apparently I had colored something terribly wrong. For my mother walked by me one day, screaming, "I will not have a left-handed child," as she jerked the crayon from my left hand and inserted it into my right.

Quite naturally, then, when I reached for the next crayon with my left hand, she quickly popped it with her right hand. This became the opening skirmish of a lasting battle about which of the two hands would become my dominant one.

When I carried a drinking glass in my stronger left hand, she instructed me to put it down and pick it up again with my right hand. As a result, I began to see my right hand as the epitome of everything that was wrong with me. If I lifted a glassful of juice to my mouth, it would often hit the floor before I could take so much as a single sip. This in turn led to more of my mother's fits of rage. Labeling me as the clumsy child, her threadbare maxim—"Use this hand and not that hand"—hit an all-time high when I reached age seven.

* * *

In due time, my sister and I began doing chores. My mother decided I was old enough to iron clothes for the family. For a beginner, it was easier to iron a large item than a small one. So one day she called me over to the ironing board where she placed a pair of her jeans. As she talked me through safely lifting the hot iron and carefully moving the jeans to press new areas, I foresaw myself easily gaining the confidence it would take to accomplish the task. And like anyone else, I did what came naturally.

I picked up the hot iron and set about smoothing out the wrinkles, gliding back and forth first with the right hand and then with the left. Having finished, I called my mother back into the room to see my progress and applaud my effort.

"Good job!" she said, as she signaled me to continue.

As I did so, still switching from the right hand to left, she suddenly rounded the corner again and shouted, "Andrea!"

Startled by the sound of her voice, my instant reflex caused me to drop the iron, which immediately fell on my leg and scorched my bare skin. I screeched in pain.

Running to assess the damage, for the only time I ever heard her say it, my mother said, "I'm sorry!"—at which point she scurried to the kitchen to retrieve some butter that according to an old wives' tale would soothe and heal the burn, which of course it didn't.

Within minutes the burn had bubbled up into a blister that stretched from the inner to the outer edge of my thigh as if I had been branded by a curling iron.

Being all the more worried by my yelping, my mother called my aunt, her next-door neighbor, who came immediately and examined the wound and advised that I should be confined to the couch for the rest of the day.

Robbed of my strength by incessant pain, I eventually fell asleep. Upon awakening but not remembering exactly why I had been on the couch in the first place, I moved about, grazing my festering thigh against the couch, causing the blister to break and ooze so that my howls set off an instant alarm in my mother's brain as she bolted forth and shouted, "That's what you get! I told you to sit down!"

Five inches wide and three inches thick, that wound remains as the painful reminder of a child who was burned, not nearly to the degree of a hot iron as to the feverous hatred of a mother who chased away the light of God, so that when this child walked, she stumbled and bumped into walls and tumbled down stairs and could no longer find her way home.

7

Salvation One Night

F rom the age of five until I was twenty-five, people often said
to me, "You have an old soul." In my youth, I did not understand what they meant or how to receive it. But during my early
twenties, while attending university, I discovered that possessing
an old soul signified the wisdom I had gained through the trials
and hardships that eventually opened my eyes to the dysfunctional
environment in which I had lived.

I remember the day she brought it into the house. My mother
walked in, called my sister and me to the living room, and said she
wanted to discuss something very important.

She had purchased what she thought was a tool of protection.
When she removed it from its green case, at first sight it appeared
as lustrous as black midnight reflecting the sheen of the shimmer-
ing white moon. In actuality, it was a weapon of destruction. Her
instruction was clear. "Never touch it!"

Every child since the beginning of time has fallen into the
parental trap of "Do not touch!" For, within a split second, the
wheels of a child's mind start turning: "How can I touch it without getting caught?"

* * *

Days went by as if nothing was wrong. From the outside of our house and looking in, most would have thought it was a great place for me to live and grow up. But within it, given my mother's repeated rejections combined with the mortal effects of the boy's sexual assault, I felt murdered little by little each day.

My demonic thoughts sprouted like seeds from the devil's soil: "She hates you, so you can hate her, too."

After weeks of replaying that mantra to myself, reinforcing how filthy, unworthy, and guilty I felt for having kept his dirty secret, on top of her failure to protect me, I heard myself repeating, "You didn't yell at him to stop! In fact, when he enticed you into that silent back bedroom, you went willingly."

Sleepless night after sleepless night I tossed and turned. How despicable and disgusting it was that time and again I returned to his disgraces, for he had ravished my childhood for the rest of my life. I cried out in silence as my tears fell into a wet pool on my pillow.

I knew well enough the names of God and Jesus from the church services I had attended, and from the children's songs I had sung, like "Jesus Loves Me." So, as I lay on my bed at the age of seven in untold agony, I called out to Jesus and implored him.

"If you truly love me, don't let me wake up tomorrow."

* * *

To my surprise, I woke up the next morning. At first, I was angry, but then the words I had memorized came back to mind.

"Jesus loves me! this I know, For the Bible tells me so. Little ones to Him belong; They are weak but He is strong. Yes, Jesus loves me, Yes, Jesus loves me, Yes, Jesus loves me, The Bible tells me so."

So I asked Jesus to prove his love for me.

But my infantile request went unanswered. So I spent another day doing battle with the Enemy hiding in darkness, seeking to convince me just how terrible a person I was.

That night, once again, I asked Jesus to prove his love for me. I prayed to God, "Maybe you didn't hear me last night, but I ask you, if you really love me, please don't let me wake up tomorrow."

Night after night for months on end I prayed that prayer to no avail. It seemed that no one was listening. So I decided to take matters into my own hands.

Trying to think of the easiest way to leave my life behind me, I pictured myself putting a plastic bag over my head, lying down, and never greeting the day again. But then, that would be too noisy and might tip off my mother or sister.

I considered drinking some of the chemicals that lay beneath the bathroom sink. But all I could think of was the directive about not touching or ingesting them.

So, how could I harm myself so that I would never be harmed again? And then a glorious revelation struck me.

The gun.

I imagined the burst of light coming from its muzzle as I contemplated firing it to set myself free. So I began to plot how to use it.

How sweet to go to sleep and rest forever, no more to be plagued by inner darkness.

* * *

Then one particular day after my mother had punished me for some trivial transgression, suddenly a new design emerged for achieving my fantasy. I not only wanted to end my suffering; I also wanted to increase hers as much as possible. But how to accomplish it?

First, I thought of shooting her and then shooting myself. But later I realized that her suffering would last only a second, which wasn't long enough to deliver the justice she deserved for constantly having tortured me with her words and her belt.

Next, I thought of shooting her in the foot just before shooting myself, which meant that for years to come with every step she took she would remember the miserable life she had created for me. But then it occurred to me that she would be far more preoccupied with her own misery than with the suffering of the child of her womb who had lain bleeding on the floor in front of her. So that wouldn't work either.

As each day came and went, my preoccupation as an eight-year-old was consumed with unworkable strategies to bring about my death and her demise. Nothing I could think of insured her downfall. I could not foresee how to fit the gun into my plan.

But then it dawned on me. I needed to retrieve the gun one night in order to feel the weight of it and practice how to hold it, and carefully place it back in the case just as I found it, so as not to alert anyone.

Then the second night I would locate the bullets and load the gun. In the meantime, I would write a letter to my mother, explaining why I chose to take my life in order to cause her to suffer. I would place the letter on her dresser just before pulling the trigger. And I would fire the gun in such a way as to splatter my brain fragments across her face.

Bone fragments and blood stains on her face were the singularly most indispensable detail for effecting my strategy. For then, every time she looked in the mirror she would stare at the marks of my revenge or else never look in the mirror again.

These were the heinous thoughts that brought a grim smile to my face as I reenacted the fantasy again and again in my haste to die. I no longer looked for light in the darkness. I wholeheartedly embraced the darkness.

But amid all my ruminating, I'd forgotten something. I'd forgotten the other people around me who would suffer as well. I was not thinking of my sister walking through my blood stains soaking the floor. I was not considering my grandfather, my father, my aunts, my uncles, and the rest of my family staring at my mutilated remains in a child-size coffin.

I had forgotten them all. I was thinking only of myself and putting an end to *my* misery.

* * *

One night, I lay awake after a particularly challenging day at school and at home. The darkness continued to devour me. The nocturnal image of those bloody-sharp teeth returned, circling about me. Every evil thought I had toward my mother boomeranged, eating away at my flesh and spirit. If only I could make the darkness disappear and end my pain forever. If only.

Lying on my bed with my face to the ceiling and tears pouring from my eyes, suddenly I heard a voice speak out of the silence— an unfamiliar but consoling voice. He asked me but one question: "Do you want me to take the darkness from you?"

Instantly, I screamed, "Yes!"

I do not know if my outcry was audible or not, but I definitely know it was "Yes!"

Mysteriously, I saw him open an enormous black garbage bag and take hold of the teeth swirling around me, and hurl them in. The teeth left no puncture marks upon him. When he turned back toward me, light shone from his eyes into mine.

Before leaving, he said, "If you need me to come back, I will."

So, the very next night when darkness threatened me yet again, I called for him once more. And faithfully he returned and took hold of the darkness and dismantled it.

What he did for me was what the saints meant when they spoke of their salvation. He redeemed me from the hell that had besieged me.

The next morning, I encountered my mother.

But I no longer looked upon her with hatred. Rather, I saw only her pain.

* * *

Unlike some, I did not receive my salvation in a church before an altar surrounded by worshippers speaking in tongues.

No organ played an upbeat rhythm to usher in the Spirit.

No pastor employed some clever scare tactic to lure me into his presence to moan and groan and weep and gnash my teeth.

My salvation arose from heaven that night, and came before me to give me life and to remove my sin—my desire to hate and kill for revenge.

From that time on, I chose to walk in love because Jesus had loved me when, consumed by darkness and death, I could not love myself.

And to this day, I still say what I deeply believe.

"Jesus loves me, This I know."

8

Rebellion

Though my heart was providentially transformed that night during what for me was a Damascus Road encounter, my stubborn willfulness would take a long time to change. In school, among peers, my life was simple. I went to class, I did my work, I ate my lunch, and I returned home. For me, academics were effortless. I was a gifted learner. Yet my behavior kept me from being labeled as socially gifted.

As for the academics, I was not a typical little backwoods country girl. By age four I had learned to read, and I excelled at writing. My sister, on the other hand, struggled during her first few years of school. Although I was several years behind her, I quickly surpassed her academically.

I was the student that teachers often fail to challenge enough to keep busy and out of trouble. In a futile attempt to do so, some offered me additional worksheets, but I completed them before the teachers could finish their own work. Some realized that giving me brain puzzles for entertainment was more productive. For those teachers I cut some slack by listening and obeying, saving my misbehavior for the playground. When bored, I became dangerous. My idle mind was the devil's workshop.

During the third grade, my parents became aware of my rebelliousness. Our teacher, who had previously taught kindergarten, didn't motivate us with challenging classwork or appropriate homework. So after about three weeks my mother insisted upon speaking with the teacher about it. Yet the teacher refused to listen to my mother, who in this instance was correct. Since I'd already mastered the spelling of three-letter and four-letter words, there was no reason to repeat those assignments. As it turned out, that teacher lasted only another month.

* * *

Our subsequent teacher, Mrs. Payne, arrived on the scene without a clue as to what she was in for. She immediately set out to give us third-grade work and yet we wanted nothing of it. We'd already developed cliques and determined the degree of effort we'd give to assignments. Lazy was the name of our game.

Some days the entire class refused to do any work, and other days just enough to get by to be eligible to go out for recess. The work itself was not difficult. The principle of the matter boiled down to our need to be headstrong. But then, when we received our report cards, the chickens came home to roost. Suddenly, we had to make some decisions. So we called together a council meeting on the playground.

One choice was to destroy the report cards and to say that we never received them. This seemed unacceptable, however, because we knew our parents would call the school to ask why there were no report cards.

Option two was more plausible, we thought. We would alter our grades by turning F's and D's into B's in the hope that our parents wouldn't notice the change. Since our report cards were handwritten, this seemed feasible. What we didn't realize was that our teacher had made a preemptive strike. She had called ahead to all of the parents before we received our report cards and thus before we could show them to our parents. Consequently, we were shocked when we arrived at our homes that afternoon.

About all I could say was, "Well-played, Mrs. Payne, well-played! You beat us to it."

* * *

The school office informed me on my way to the school bus that I should return home and not go to the babysitter's house as was my usual routine. When the bus pulled up in front of my house, I noticed that the front door was slightly ajar. I could not see anyone through the glass but I could tell that I was about to enter dangerous territory. My nerves stood on edge as I walked up the driveway. My heart raced as I ascended the three steps to the front porch door. I knew I was in trouble.

My fears were confirmed. My mother was sitting on the couch with a belt in her hand and with fury in her eyes.

"Put your backpack down and get over here," she demanded.

Oh, how I wished I had had the courage to run away. Seconds later the spanking commenced. My behind took the brunt of her onslaught, more so than the back of my legs.

Our encounter was like round one of a heavyweight boxing match that concluded with a sudden knockout. I was defeated so rapidly and badly that I didn't have the strength to cry. My mother ranted and raved, unleashing her anger as she sent me off to bed.

It was only 4 p.m., but I quietly walked my pain-ridden body down the hallway to my bedroom and slept.

After resting from the Tyson vs. Holyfield remake, my mother woke me from my slumber and called me to the front of the house. In my naïveté I was thinking she wanted to discuss her expectations of me in school. But to my surprise she was sitting in her familiar position on the couch, ready for battle. Round two of our heavyweight match was about to begin.

During the time I had been asleep, she had stewed some more about my behavior at school and the embarrassment I had caused her. So, once again, she unleashed her fury on my backside. Only later did I learn that she had gone through my

35

backpack and discovered the handwritten letter grades that I had penciled next to the official ones.

The fact was that, ever since being in the first grade, I had received but one grade on my report cards—a straight A in all subjects—in addition to being on the principal's list, with my name announced on the public address system and published in the local newspaper.

My relatives always called to congratulate me, and my mother was full of pride whenever she heard what others spoke of me. I obtained a reputation in my family for being the child with "book smarts." And yet some accused me of lacking street smarts. Little did they know, however, just how quickly I had acquired those skills as well.

So, on this particular night, as she looked over my actual grades, she saw *Reading, F; Math, F; Science, F; Social Studies, D;* and *Writing, F.*, which re-ignited her fury to the extent that the belt she applied to my backside felt like red-hot flames scorching the seat of my pants.

Unfortunately for me, that was not the end of the torture.

* * *

We awoke early the next morning and headed out of the house, together with my sister, for the dreaded parent-teacher conference that I had completely forgotten about. After waiting outside the classroom, the teacher welcomed us to come in and sit around a small table.

My mother first of all apologized for my lack of effort and reassured the teacher that the situation had been rectified. Then, without speaking a word, my mother glared at me with eyes that did all the talking. I knew immediately that she was signaling me to offer my apology. So I made it short and sweet.

Getting down to business, the teacher spoke highly of my verbal ability and provocative answers to questions. Yet she also explained that I did not apply the same aptitude to my written assignments.

My mother looked down at me and asked, "Why?"

After a moment of silence she pressed the point again. "Why?"

I felt like giving her a slick answer by saying that the work was stupid, but I quickly thought I had better not. Given the bruising my rear-end had already suffered, I bound my tongue.

What my mother didn't know at the time was that I had completed all of the assignments but hadn't turned them in to the teacher.

She stood up and casually walked over to my desk, opened it, and rifled through the jumbled mess. Repeatedly glancing up at me, she pulled out my notebooks and some of my completed work. After unfolding and smoothing out the papers, she brought them back to the table.

She asked the teacher to show her the gradebook and the assignments for which I had received a zero, which accounted for all of the papers in the stack that my mother was holding.

I could feel her temperature rising as she realized that the zeros were due to my rebelliousness. She then pled with the teacher to check for all of the work that I failed to complete in future grading periods. The teacher agreed to do so and looked over at me and said matter-of-factly, "Only work placed in the basket for completed assignments would be graded in the future." I nodded that I understood.

My mother thanked the teacher while simultaneously applying the "church pinch" to my arm as we exited the room. On the way to the car we had a serious conversation about my new to-do list, and she threatened my life if I ever again forgot to turn in even one assignment.

I believed her. My prideful attitude, masquerading as open rebellion, had been duly humbled.

I had raw flesh to show for it.

9

Clothing

When getting ready for school in the morning during my elementary years, a colorful dress or a designer t-shirt and bottoms, along with matching shoes and socks, awaited me on the couch as I came from the bathroom.

At that time, little brown girls wore hair balls in coordinating colors known by various names: bow knockers, bow balls, twisters, knobs, or hair balls. Finding the right one was the last step in dressing to leave the house.

Part of growing up was gaining the independence with which to pick out our own clothes. Parents generally determined when their children were ready to assume that responsibility, which for me was age five.

During the first week of September, stores had extravagant sales to entice parents to purchase new outfits for the start of the school year. Many parents who awaited their next paycheck dreaded the fact that it reminded them of their own poverty in contrast to the wealth of others. Their children didn't get the stylish labels and name-brands. They wore whatever their parents could afford, but this wasn't the case for my sister and me.

My mother insisted that we each start the school year with one pair of white sneakers and one pair of black. We were allowed to buy seven pairs of pants, fourteen shirts, and a few skirts and dresses for our annual wardrobe.

As a five-year-old, I did not understand the value of money in relation to the cost of goods. A week after school had begun one year, I had not yet worn my white shoes. My mother insisted that I do so because she said they looked much better with the outfit that I planned to wear.

But I did not like high-top Reeboxes. So on the way home from school I threw one of them out the car window. My mother did not realize what I had done in that moment. Upon arriving home, she noticed that I was carrying but one shoe. To put it mildly, she was furious. As I hobbled into the house, she lit into me with a harsh spanking.

Even though I was tempted, I never again littered the road by tossing something out of the window. My mother also learned a valuable lesson, which was never to buy me a pair of shoes that I clearly disliked.

* * *

When the day came for me to take responsibility for choosing my own attire, I readily learned the importance of looking cute before leaving the house. Eventually, I was able to mix and match different tops and pants, as well as not mix polka dots with stripes and plaids.

By the time I reached late elementary and early middle school, my parents were concerned with only one thing—the price tag. The style and appropriateness of each article became insignificant. And that was the beginning of my madness. For some, name brands were triple the cost of generic labels, with shoes and sneakers being among them. Even though my sister and I were expected to spend $500 on shoes alone, clever marketing and peer pressure had sucked us into thinking that the labels were necessary. Since fearing a harmless joke spoken in ridicule might reduce us to feeling like we were less than nothing, we opted for the more expensive items.

"How are the boys going to view me?" soon became my principal question. I was built like one of my great-aunts, cute in the face, thin in the waist, thick in the thighs, and blessed in the behind. So when I wore a cute dress, the boys naturally commented on how attractive I looked. The shorter the dress, the more the boys took notice, up to the point that the burn on my thigh from the ironing incident became my measuring line for shortness.

Like many fourteen-year-old girls, I became addicted to attention, that is, until some of the boys thought that my evocative dress meant that my body was free for their feeling. Even some of the men tossed cat-calls and come-on lines my way.

* * *

Teenage boys often gave attention to the girls desiring attention, in order to get something in return. I soon realized that they wanted more than a compliment. When my clothes were a bit skimpy, I received two or three kisses a day, even though I couldn't enjoy them because of the grotesque taste of smoke and alcohol on their breath.

On the other hand, I desired kisses from the super cute boys. By age sixteen, I was a pro at kissing when I was enticed. Yet, very soon, kissing lips became fondling hands, and before I knew it we had gone too far.

I experienced firsthand what it meant to grow up too soon. With my hormones raging and my physical responses increasingly addicted, I spent too much time with boys, unchaperoned.

Being a student in the American public school system guaranteed two things: First, that students were grouped among peers based upon their equivalent age rather than their economic background, race, ethnicity, or religion; and second, that exposure to sex education came far too early.

I remember my first sex education class in the third grade. We were divided into two groups, male and female. The teachers led us into separate rooms to watch a film. I had never before asked any questions about the anatomy of boys. But, as a result of the film, I became extremely curious. The playground suddenly became the place to find a boy with whom to ask questions, some of those questions being more intimate than others.

As an adult looking back at photos of myself as a teenager, my first thought was, where were my parents? My shorts were so short as to be hardly more than underwear. My shirts barely covered my cleavage.

Had my parents never taught me the value of each precious part of my body? Had my sex education classes not emphasized the importance of keeping precious what should always remain precious? Apparently not.

Who then recognized the early signs that my life was heading into a downward spiral?

If anyone, certainly it was not I.

10

A Fight to End the Fighting

Americans value strong and independent women, and my mother was the epitome. She worked full time, raised two children of her own, paid a mortgage, and supported the lifestyle she desired. But early on, when her mother was diagnosed with breast cancer, her life and her goals abruptly shifted.

The cancer diagnosis necessitated pausing her college career in order to enter the workforce full-time, even though she was engaged to be married and planned to have children in the hope that her mother could enjoy being a grandmother. But while carrying a new life in her womb, she experienced the heartbreak of seeing her mother's life decline until the day when, face-to-face with the frailty of life and the finality of death, her mother drew her last breath and departed this earth.

I often heard stories about my grandmother's life. She, too, was a strong and independent woman. Those who knew her best sometimes described her as "mean and vicious." As an overseer in the company for which she worked—an uncommon position for a woman, especially a Black woman—she commanded a "troop" of men and women to follow her orders as they readied a product for nationwide marketing. Her own family also knew what it was like to be on the receiving end of her strict discipline. Not only did she work full-time, but she also managed a household of two daughters, two sons, and a husband. My mother, who was second in the birth order, learned by observation and experience what it meant to be strong and independent.

* * *

My mother's sadness turned into joy on the Christmas Eve shortly after my grandmother's death, her grief eased as she gave birth to my older sister. But the expectation of a home filled with the love and laughter of a happy couple nurturing a newly born baby girl became short-lived as my parents' marital discord increased.

The house went uncleaned, the laundry piled up, unwashed dishes overflowed the kitchen sink, and, to top it off, the baby cried throughout the night. After a few months, the pressures of living together, working and parenting, forged an insurmountable barrier between the two of them. He, who felt that being at home was like carrying the weight of a high-rise building on his back, found solace at work where in comparison his responsibilities were light. She, feeling ever more distressed and burdened by all that transpired both day and night, searched for love and affection outside of the house.

One day, heartbroken, she discovered evidence of his infidelity. By having married a man who didn't live up to his commitment to love, cherish, and forsake all others, giving himself to her alone, she had let herself down as the strong and independent woman she once had been. With his marriage vows but shards of broken promises, she quickly turned her heartbreak into rage.

When he arrived home from work after the midnight shift, she waited for him without going to bed. Pulling into the driveway, he noticed the lights were on in the house, which usually meant that the baby was awake.

As he stepped out of the car, he saw the front door swing open in a gust of fury. Thinking that something had gone seriously wrong, he was stunned to see armfuls of his clothing hurled out the door and flying onto the front lawn.

From her incoherent shouts he quickly realized that she had found the damning evidence of his extra-marital affair. Desperately, but to no avail, he tried to explain that he had not been unfaithful to her, but that whenever he had not been at home or work, he had been visiting his sick father. Yet the time for engaging in rational conversation had expired, and any further attempts at reasoning would only infuriate her all the more. So he turned around and left.

* * *

Here was a beautiful and intelligent woman, a new wife and new mother, reduced to a fit of rage, spinning out of control, and barely hanging on for dear life.

So one night, her estranged husband decides to return home in an effort to reconcile their relationship. And what does he find?

He finds her in the house he had built for her, lying in the arms of another man. So now the tables were turned, and he was the one spouting fury. Instead of wanting to reconcile the marriage, he was angry enough to burn the whole place down.

Both of them now stood on the same side of wrong, with their new accomplices acting like pawns in the marital game of chess. Could things possibly get any worse?

A few months after the double affairs were exposed, my mother discovered that she was pregnant. She chose to share the news with no one except her best friend who happened to be expecting a third child herself. The two mothers were to share the same expected delivery date.

But an important question lingered. Who was the true father of my mother's second child?—a question that many women wish never to have to ask. Was it a child by her husband or a child by her lover?

The dark secret remained hidden in broad daylight, disguised by oversized clothes and the blessing of appearing to carry a small fetus in the womb.

So the day for the delivery arrived without anyone in her family expecting to receive the phone call that set the entire grapevine abuzz. "The baby is here, and it's a girl!" she declared.

A boatload of questions raced through her mind.

Who should I call to accompany me to the hospital?

What last name ought this child to possess?

How will my family respond?

Will he come if I call him?

Is she even his child to begin with?

11

I Am More Like You
Than You Think

The pain of childbirth must have cleared a path through her mind. For she knew to call and inform the man she once had loved and now despised, the man who was her husband in title only, who had shown no responsibility throughout the pregnancy.

Upon arrival at the hospital, she was told that the baby in her womb was premature and that there might be some complications with the delivery. Despite this, she forged ahead and delivered a five-pound three-ounce bundle of joy—which was me.

Calls went out as the news spread quickly to her family and his. She named the baby in accordance with their little family tradition of giving their children the same initials.

So there they were, husband and wife, he having just found out that he might have fathered another daughter, and she wondering what to do next.

The quarrels surrounding their newborn child became epic. She often called the police, not because he had physically or mentally harmed her, but simply as a weapon by which to demean and destroy him. They debated when he could see the children. They argued about clothes, hair, what the children ate, where they slept, and with whom they spent their time. Spending it with relatives presented a frequent point of contention for all parties concerned.

* * *

Eventually my father had had enough. He decided to appeal to the court to obtain visitation rights with both of us. We, the children, and the judge, were witnesses to the marital warfare. It was during those visits to the courthouse that I experienced my earliest resentments toward my mother.

When I was eight years old my mother married her second husband. Life settled down when he entered. He was a welcomed distraction. But they were not satisfied with the two children in the house already, for they wanted a child of their own.

She announced her pregnancy to us a year after they were married. The entire family was excited to hear the news that our family was growing. But soon after the announcement of a new life, there came the devastating news that she was experiencing a miscarriage. At the time I did not understand what that meant, but I did know that she would not be bringing the baby home from the hospital with her.

A few months later she explained to my sister and me again that she was expecting another baby. This time they waited to announced it to the family. When she was about five months pregnant, she informed the family that they were expecting a baby boy.

The bouncing baby boy joined what seemed like a happy family. There was only one problem. His mother was experiencing postpartum symptoms and could not care for her baby most of the time. So it was left to the rest of us in the house to make sure he was fed, bathed, carried around, and cuddled. He was a sweet baby, so we all fought to care for him. He was well loved.

It became a nightly routine for my sister and me to take turns trying to get him to sleep. We spent hours walking him up and down the hallway in his stroller to get him to doze off. I read him the same books so often that I had memorized them. We washed his bottles, laundered his clothes, and entertained him to keep him quiet.

He was, figuratively speaking, my first baby. I learned many things to do and not to do with my little brother, the first of which was to say to myself, "Do not sit and hold the baby all day or else you will not be able to put that child down even when you have important things to do." In our family he was affectionately named a lap-baby, meaning he needed to be seated in someone's lap all the time.

* * *

As I grew older, my animosity toward my mother only increased. By the time I was sixteen, it was painfully obvious that we were not meant to live under the same roof. Our conflicts and confrontations were physical, mental, and emotional. More than once the police were called.

One day, after an incident, one of my aunts telephoned my mother to ask if I could move in with her family. My mother responded indignantly with a few curse words and then hung up the phone. How dare anyone insinuate that she could not manage her own children. She was appalled at the thought that someone else might have reason to raise the one she could not control.

Most of our mutual hostility and frustration stemmed from the fact that, as part of my maturation, I wanted to exercise certain appropriate controls that she refused to relinquish. After many contentious episodes, my father's girlfriend also noticed the further decline of my relationship with my mother. Consequently, just as my aunt had done, she put forth the same request for me to come live with her, which of course was denied.

* * *

When I was around sixteen, I reached my breaking point. So I decided that my mother needed a taste of her own medicine, which sparked the worst period of rebellion in my life. Virtually everything became a reason to engage in combat. The cause or effect of an argument didn't matter so long as the battle ensued.

If she said, "Go to bed," then I stayed up a few more hours, no matter how tired I was. If she said, "Wash the dishes!" then I left the kitchen uncleaned for several days. Since I was the sole dishwasher in the house, the sink remained inundated with dirty dishes as we ate our way around the mess.

"Pick up your brother from the school bus!" led to one of the worst of our battles. Instead of agreeing to do so, I stood up and told my mother that I would be staying after school, and that I would call social services to let them know that my brother had been abandoned.

My comment infuriated her. She lunged at me as I stood with my feet planted firmly on the floor in front of her in my bedroom doorway. I instantly informed her that there would be no more beatings, and that if a physical altercation occurred, it would be a fight to the finish.

As she raised her hand to strike me, I slammed the bedroom door in her face and locked it. I picked up the phone and dialed 9-1-1.

The police soon arrived to take our statements about the incident. They informed her not to hit me and told me not to engage in any form of dispute with her, which ended it for the night but not for good.

A week later, none of her laundry had been washed because, practically speaking, I had thrown the chore chart out the window.

So early one morning, my mother came into my room looking for something to wear to work. She found an outfit hanging on my door and proceeded to take it. When my alarm clock chimed and woke me from sleep, I exited the bed, went to the bathroom, showered, and returned to my room to get dressed.

Glancing at my door, I discovered that the clothes I had chosen were missing. And I was furious!

So what did I do? I did the only thing a teenager filled with anger and rage could think to do, which was to plot my payback.

I took an armful of my mother's clothes from her laundry hamper and tossed them into the washer, with all of the fabrics and colors mixed together without discrimination. The more the mixture of colors, the better.

I closed the lid to the washing machine and set the temperature to hot. I reopened the lid, added laundry detergent, bleach, and fabric softener all together, and let the machine do its job. I knew the result would be disastrous. Shirts, pants, skirts, socks, panties, and scarves, all destroyed in one load.

I was so fueled with rage that I didn't even think of the consequences. My mind, like that of many a hormonal teen, was set on the here and now, not on the repercussions.

As for my mother and our long-standing, bitter conflict—looking back from the perspective of these many years and considerable experience—I would humbly need to say to her quite simply, "I am more like you than you think."

12

My First Encounter

In schools across America, peer pressure about academics, drugs, alcohol, and sex can be quite intense, affecting every aspect of a student's life in the present and for the future. Parental pressures can complicate the picture. Some parents drive their children to achieve in order to compensate for the fact that they did not. The combination of peer and parental pressure can feel like multiple assaults coming from every direction, including from male students pressuring female students to respond to sexual advances. In the hallway, on the bus, in the classroom, and during lunch break, girls suffer from the ever-present expectation that their popularity depends upon engaging in some form of sexual activity with their male counterparts.

I remember being about age fifteen when a guy in the neighborhood said that I was too "energetic." At the time, I did not understand what he meant. In his mind I was still playful like a child on a playground or a kid in the candy store. I had always been proud of my virginity, which to me was a treasured jewel. I did not believe that being molested counted as a pleasurable experience. However, his remark caused me to question my previous assumptions about teenage sex.

Conversations among students, whether on the school bus or the football field, often turned to the subject of who was sexually active. Teens occasionally revealed details about their personal sexual activity. Yet few of us had a sense for how our teenage sexual adventures might affect us for the rest of our lives. Like many in the broader society, we considered sexual intercourse to be recreational. At school we were taught to engage in safe sex by protecting our bodies with the use of condoms and birth control. Yet no one stopped to mention how to protect our hearts, minds, and spirits.

In the early 1990s, during the HIV crisis, we heard persistent warnings about the dangers of contracting the virus. Images of those suffering and dying from AIDS terrified us. Fear of the disease discouraged premature sex. Yet fear alone was seldom sufficient to frighten hormonal teens from giving in to a ravenous sexual appetite.

Sometimes fear of the disease, coupled with anxiety about an unwanted pregnancy, had an inhibiting effect. The idea of walking around for nine months with everyone staring at you dissuaded some girls from risking pregnancy. But others succumbed to the relentless daily onslaught of the boys.

* * *

One day in the ninth grade, my teacher spoke with the class about the historical importance of sex. He explained that since cave dwellers didn't possess books, TV, or radio, the only thing they had left to do after a day's work in the wild was to engage in sex. That's how they populated the earth.

But what he failed to say was that, despite all the modern-day distractions, including video games, cell phones, apps, blogs, vlogs, books, and movies, we are no less likely to engage in sex than the caveman who asked the cavewoman, "What shall we do after supper tonight?" and she answered, "You clean up the venison scraps and I'll put the kids to bed."

In those days, the cave consisted of rock walls, a dirt floor, and fire heating up the air. In today's world, the cave consists of sheet rock, a wooden floor, and fire heating up the queen-size bed to the tune of Beyoncé's "Crazy in Love." And that's why, historically speaking, there are more people in today's world than there were way back then.

So the issue is that we are surrounded by sex no matter which way we turn. And because I was never one to undertake an action without at least contemplating the consequences, I normally did a cost-benefit analysis in my head and then decided whether or not to proceed. If I was willing to accept the consequences, then I moved forward and welcomed my fate.

As I looked around at the teen girls in my school, swooning over the boys as they moved up and down the hallway, I knew I didn't want to be like them. Some of the boys were my closest friends. I heard them talk about passing girls from one boy to another. If only those girls had known how the boys dragged their names through the mud, they would have chosen to keep their legs closed. A wise woman once told me, "Never date a boy who goes to the same school as you." It was some of the best advice I ever received about dating while still in high school.

So I developed a mission. I determined I would find a boy I deemed worthy. My requirements were that he must be attractive but not drop-dead gorgeous, smart but not a genius, strong but not a brute, and kind but not a pushover. He must be at least all of these and hopefully more. So off I went, hunting for "him."

One day, when I was out and about with a family, I heard a young man speaking in a kindly voice. Despite his being a teenager, he was physically full-grown and had a seriousness about him, in addition to an authentically contagious laugh. Observing him closely I noticed that he spoke sweet and kind words to the women around him. He mentioned that the last days of his senior year were the happiest of his life. The more I heard, the more I wanted to know. Before long, a mutual friend introduced us.

But I wondered. Were his kind words genuinely reflective of his personality, or were they deceptive?

When he looked at me with some of the deepest and darkest chocolate eyes I had ever seen, I felt as though he was looking through me rather than at me. Given his penetrating gaze, what was a girl to do?

Why, of course, what else but play hard to get! I wanted to find out just how much and for what purpose he would pursue me. He willingly accepted the challenge.

In small talk typical of a budding relationship, he began by asking basic questions about me. Then he proceeded to tell me about wonderful things he wanted to accomplish with his life, things that were neither lofty nor particularly exciting. He didn't aspire to change the world. He simply wished to live a normal life. We spoke for twenty minutes and then re-entered the conversation with other teens.

For the remainder of the evening I watched him from across the room. Whenever he laughed, I wanted to hear him laugh again. Whenever he smiled, I thought I just might feel comfortable being with him. Before we departed, he asked me for my phone number.

* * *

A few days later the phone rang. It was the voice I was waiting to hear. We proceeded to play the twenty-question phone game that required simple answers with little to no thought. We asked each other about birthdays, favorite colors, and TV shows. Then we turned to the subject of our families and how they either helped or hindered us, which led to describing what kind of a family we wanted for ourselves someday. We talked for an hour.

Over the next few weeks we spoke by phone nearly every night. We watched the same TV programs simultaneously so that we could share moments of laughter and sadness together. We spoke of the day's events at school. And though we lived in different cities, our experiences were quite similar—boys flirting with girls, girls gossiping about other girls, and fights breaking out in the hallways between bells.

In time, a giant elephant entered the room—namely, sex—but we never discussed it. This was despite my having already decided that he was the one to whom I would give my precious gem. I felt that I could trust him to cherish and care for it. He would never make a billboard out of me nor share his prized possession at a football game. His kind spirit, gentle demeanor, and trusting hands were worthy of my confidence and assured me that he would not hurt me.

Having no fear about asking awkward questions, the time came to find out if he had ever shared his body with anyone else. I needed to know what risks there might be in having sex with him. So I inquired about HIV. He said that he had tested negative. Then I posed the harder question about how many partners he had had. I needed to know how crowded the bed might be, should we decide to get in it together. The number was small, which increased my sense of feeling safe with him since he didn't appear to be a reckless bed hopper. Then, too, he didn't want children, which meant I could trust him to protect both of us from that possibility.

The fact is that I was betting. I was betting on a mighty act of rebellion—my own—which prompted another question: Was he, or was he not, the one with whom to share this once-in-a-lifetime special moment?

Each night as I lay in bed I thought of the reasons why I should, and the reasons why I shouldn't, carry through with my intention. But no matter how cautious I was in weighing the costs and benefits of the decision, the five-year-old rebel in me was still very much alive in this fifteen-year-old body.

After three weeks of talking myself into having sex with him, but not sharing it with another living soul, I developed my strategic plan.

I calculated how long it would take my mother to get home from work, then pick up my brother from soccer practice and buy dinner before returning home. On average that would take from two to two and a half hours. So, to be safe, I planned an hour and forty-five minutes for our sexual encounter, factoring in my clean-up time and the clearance of his departure.

But there was one thing left to figure out. Do I tell him that I am still a virgin? Would informing him scare him away? Might he be willing to participate in my rebellious ploy if he knew of my virginity in advance?

And then—if I had held onto my precious gem for fifteen years, then why was I so willing to give it away now?

The answer was simple: *rebellion and revenge.*

So I finally decided not to tell him until it was literally too late to back out.

* * *

Parents fail to realize that "do as I say, not as I do" parenting does not work. My level of disdain for my mother had reached an all-time high. She loved to portray herself and her family as perfect to the outside world. A perfect house, a perfect husband, and perfect children all living happily under one roof was how she perceived her family. But for those of us living on the inside it was a totally different story.

My mother, after divorcing my father, had married my stepfather. And now the two of them were on the brink of a divorce. My sister and I were engaged in adult activities without their guidance, and my little brother was being raised by the television.

Bills were barely being paid. Chores were hardly getting done. And love was a word never heard within the walls of the house.

I wanted to destroy the false image that my mother so desperately wanted to convey. So off I went on the path of retribution, not realizing that in the process I was destroying a valuable part of myself.

I called to inform him that I would have the house to myself for a few hours and that he should stop by. He had never been inside. He had only picked me up out front or from the school bus stop. With excitement in his voice he agreed to make the journey.

Everyone knew that when a girl invited a boy over to her house while her parents were away, it meant they were going to be engaging in some form of sex play. So here I was, joining the ranks of all those teenage girls who had gone down the primrose path in search of sensual pleasure.

On that fateful day I rushed home from school and straightaway prepared the house for him to make his grand entrance into my overheated world. I changed the bed sheets. I cleaned my closet. I organized my dresser. I removed all the knick-knacks from its top and cleared my nightstand. I went through my closet to choose the appropriate outfit for the occasion. But I couldn't find anything that I liked, so I put that decision on hold. I aerated the room with a fragrant body spray. And I doused myself with perfume from my collection. The last thing I did was to confirm the invitation with a phone call.

* * *

He rang the doorbell and I hurried down the stairs to greet him in a dress that scarcely covered my thighs.

As he walked in, we kissed at the door, which was no different than every other greeting many times before. But this time he pulled me close and held me tighter. His strong arms wrapping around me made me feel safe. I felt comfortably reassured that I had made a good decision to choose this man to be my first lover.

But, as confident as I was, I was confidently wrong. Sadly, I didn't realize it until much later in my life.

After our initial embrace, I took him by the hand and led him up the stairs, around the corner, and down the hallway to my bedroom, where I had heard his voice before by telephone, but now in his presence.

I helped him remove his jacket and tossed it onto the floor beside the bed. I lifted his shirt and assisted him in pulling it over his head. His body stood before me in all its muscularity and strength.

At that very moment I had second thoughts about proceeding with my initiation into adulthood. Would I still be able to see myself as the young lady I once considered myself to be?

But it was too late. I had already let him begin undressing me, and I didn't want to retreat in cowardice.

Moments later, pain swept through my body. Not just the pain from his penetration, but the pain of my rebellion separating me from the very God I believed in—the God who believed in me, and the God who loved me. With each thrust I felt further removed from his presence.

The treasured gift that was of such great importance to me was now defiled. I had relinquished it to a man who was not my husband. In premeditating the various repercussions, I had altogether missed seeing the lasting spiritual impact of my decision.

At the time, I did not understand the concept of a "soul tie," and yet on my bed, covered as it was with a floral comforter and white canopy, I had tied my soul and body to this man. He had done nothing to earn the privilege, and I could not retrieve what I had given him. Some gifts simply can't be returned.

I eventually learned that there is no such thing as sex without consequence. Believing otherwise was a sin, and proceeding accordingly was tampering with fire. And then operating from that delusion was simply self-deception. My first encounter became a second, and then a third, until my flesh, seeking its earthly pleasure, got wildly out of control. The cavewoman needed to quit tampering with the fire, and tamp down her uninhibited desire.

13

Baby Girl, You Were Loved but Not Wanted

My first taste of sex was exquisite and powerful. With each passing day I wanted more. At first, we made sure to protect ourselves against an unwanted pregnancy, but the novelty soon wore off, as did our diligence in taking precaution. Sex was suddenly more than recreational entertainment. We were rolling the dice to savor the sweetness of a forbidden fruit.

Soon I began drinking alcohol. Cursing had long been a part of my oration, and now I gave no regard to whom I cursed, or the location, or the audience that overheard it.

My clothing was becoming more provocative. And why shouldn't it? Or so I thought. I was an older child engaging in a grown woman's activities.

I expressed my love to him daily. We had sex at least twice a week. We talked both day and night. We hung out together just about every weekend. He was the primary focus of my attention as our lives became more and more intertwined. Life was good, until it was not.

The truth was that my life was in a rapid descent even though I couldn't see it. I was fooling myself by believing that I was in control of myself. My waywardness was increasingly intolerable. I was getting on my own nerves. I failed to listen to my inner critic when it spoke to me about fulfilling my most important commitments. I hated being at home. And increasingly I hated being in school.

* * *

Academically, I was still in honor's classes and performing above average. But if I didn't like the teacher, then I would see to it that I got kicked out of the class in order not to have to suffer through the day's lesson.

My teachers began to take notice. They observed my disrespect and my distorted view of school. However, I wanted to get good grades, which lead to my becoming a master of the art of the "cheat."

For most students, cheating consisted of a single pattern constantly repeated, which is why most who cheated got caught after a short period of time. My plan was more complex than jotting down notes on my hand or forearm. I did not hide answers in my purse or my pocket. I tailored my cheating techniques to each classroom, each teacher, and each subject.

In pre-calculus, for instance, most tests were multiple choice. This meant I needed to sit behind or beside the smarter students in order to copy their bubble sheets.

I sat behind a foreign exchange student from Germany and asked him to slouch in his chair and hold up his answer key so that I could mimic it. Then I "b—s——d" my way through the "work" to prove my mathematical reasoning, and gladly received a grade of A.

Cheating in the history class was a bit more complicated. This teacher adhered to fill-in-the-blank, true and false questions, short answers, and essays for each and every test. She made it more difficult for me to obtain an unearned A. So I developed a plan built on my relationship with other students. I waited outside the classroom door to ask someone I knew to tell me exactly what I needed to review for the test, which provided me with necessary concepts while eliminating unnecessary ones.

* * *

It was during this time that I bought clothing for the sole purpose of causing the boys to lust after my flesh. They whistled and cat-called me as I walked through the mall or down the school's hallway. While the attention I received was definitely addictive, there was also a strong part of me that yearned at times simply to wear a skirt without a single boy saying anything about it.

It was then that I began to attend church more regularly. Yet still there was a notable discrepancy between what I wore on Sunday mornings and what I wore the rest of the week. In my Pentecostal best for worship, my hems fell below my knees and over my stockings. I covered my shoulders and appropriately concealed my breasts. But the rest of the week my clothes looked more like undergarments, with shorts that could pass for boys' shorts and with tops that were cut lower than low. The best way to put it is to say that my weekday dress revealed the condition of my damaged heart as much as much it did my meagerly covered skin.

While I continued to partake of the forbidden fruit as if it would always remain ripe and ready to satisfy my ravenous sexual appetite, it also became increasingly clear to me that my cravings were every bit as destructive as they were gratifying.

To be sure, I could have died in a state of moral decline, had it not been for the fact that God was still calling my name so that I could hear a voice other than my own speaking to me from within.

* * *

Life at home was becoming more challenging and harder to manage. Given the opportunity, I would take a chance on escaping. My boyfriend at the time had a car. Finding an excuse to leave the house was my daily brain teaser. I was clever enough not to give the same reason too often, and I always had a back-up explanation in case the first one failed. Some pretexts were borderline science fiction but real enough to be believable. My mother cautiously obliged.

"I have a project with a friend due tomorrow, and I need to go to their house," I said.

"I have an after school activity every Wednesday," which was not true.

"Can I go to Walmart to look around with a friend?"

"We need milk from the store. Can I walk to go buy some?"

All of these excuses gave me at least a few hours of solitude outside of the house, long enough to slip away from my family and spend some quality time with him. We found a dark, quiet spot to engage in intercourse, and did so often, our hearts drawing closer with each rendezvous. A kind man who made me feel important and special, he made me laugh frequently as we shared inside jokes. Few people knew that we were as involved with each other as we were.

With the announcement of the school's formal dance, everyone began to prepare. I asked him if he would like to attend with me and he agreed. The night of the dance we left the party and did what we normally did by finding a dark corner for some intimacy, the only difference being that we were in formal clothing. We had long before stopped using any type of contraceptive.

When school reopened the following fall, my older sister was already six months pregnant, which caused considerable tension in the family. It also distracted everyone from what I was doing quietly in the background.

My mother had discovered my sister's pregnancy because my sister had complained of persistent back aches. The complaints prompted my mother to take her to a doctor who detected the baby growing in her womb. The back pain turned out to be from a kidney infection with the potential to jeopardize both her health and the baby's. In my mother's mind, this was sufficient reason to tell her older child to terminate the pregnancy of her unborn child, which surely made for a long ride home from the doctor's office.

That afternoon's announcement of the pregnancy caused an even greater rift in my relationship with my mother. Standing in my sister's bedroom doorway, my moyther insisted that the baby not be carried to term. As I listened from my brother's bedroom, I heard her in typical fashion assault my sister with bogus statistics about teenage death rates during pregnancy, as well as high school drop-out and infant mortality rates. Her goal was to scare my sister into agreeing to an abortion.

After fifteen minutes of listening to them, I stepped into the room and stood near my sister and vehemently said, "Keep your baby if you want it."

That statement alone was enough to infuriate my mother.

Then I told my sister that girls had babies all the time and survived, which was sufficient encouragement for her to say that she wanted to keep the baby. And for the next five months her pregnancy played out as the big scandal that it was in the family.

* * *

During this time I made sure my grades stayed above par, and I tried to kick up as little fuss as possible. I had learned early in life that a quiet mouse can sneak off with the contents of the entire refrigerator while the household is distracted. So I discreetly went about my days, sneaking under the radar, that is, until one frightening afternoon.

It was September, and I was sitting quietly in my bedroom when I heard my mother approach the door. As she walked across the threshold, she asked a question that rocked my world off its axis.

"When was the last time you had a period? I have not bought you sanitary pads in a while!"

What was I to say? That I don't know? That I don't care because I hate that period when it comes? Or, that it came last week, and that I bought the pads myself?

None of those statements was the whole truth. The first was closer to the truth in that I didn't know, yet I did care. I cared a great deal. I cared even more now that she had asked. But I could not let her see the panic on my face. I knew that it had been at least three months since the last period, and I had not had a menstrual cycle all summer.

After she left my room I jumped up and searched the calendar that I used to keep track of my cycle. I had tossed it in a drawer, which was the first clue to the fact that I had unconsciously put it out of sight to ignore it. For I was enjoying my lustful life to the fullest extent, without regard for the consequences that awaited me around the corner.

My next thought, however, was the one that changed my life forever.

"I do not want this baby," I said to myself.

Those words were so bold that I could not bring myself to utter them. Pondering them for a few moments, I remembered what had happened in school.

I had recently engaged in a few debates with those in my inner circle on the topic of abortion. I knew where I stood on the pro-choice versus pro-life argument. I knew that my beliefs were too strong for me to go against them. Even in the face of my own distressing situation, I could not succumb to the pressure to get rid of my baby. So I quickly dismissed the thought of having an abortion.

I had already made my choice. I had chosen to live outside the will of God in order to satisfy my own sexual desires, which were real, for they had stemmed from a childhood filled with sexual abuse, pornography, and a hyper-sexualized culture. The seeds of my iniquity had grown into an unquenchable urge within me to sleep with a man at all costs, and not just any man but a man of my choosing.

So my dilemma was this: Do I make the decision to abort, now that I am the one who must decide for myself? Or do I bring the baby into this world to the detriment of my future?

At that moment, I felt helpless as I thought about the unborn child in my belly. And not only helpless, but hopeless. But then I remembered.

I remembered the Man who had come to me in the dark night of my soul when I was eight, and shattered the darkness with his light. It was Jesus who had rescued me from weeping and gnashing of teeth. And I needed Him to rescue me again. So I fell to my knees and cried out to Him. And this was my prayer:

"Our Father who art in heaven, I have made a grave mistake. Please remove this bitter cup from me. I am so sorry for all the times I have sinned against you by sleeping with him. Please forgive me. And, Lord, if you get me out of this one, I promise I will never do it again."

I bargained with God.

For the next three days I spent hours on my knees by my bedside, praying, begging, pleading, and promising God anything and everything I could think of just to get Him to hear my prayer. All I wanted was for Him to remove the baby from my womb.

I don't remember eating or drinking for three days. All I recall is crying, kneeling, and praying. I saw my life going up in smoke and all my dreams vanishing into vapor. What could I do but surrender everything to God?

* * *

The third day, when I awoke from a brief but peaceful sleep, I felt the pain in my body that I had hoped to feel with every approaching hour. My thoughts returned to the first time I menstruated, when one of my aunts told me that the day would come when I would be glad to see that blood. And this was that day.

It was the most painful menstruation I'd ever experienced, having prayed for it from the depths of my heart. Finally now, a miscarriage!

Although by that time my body had developed all the signs of pregnancy, including a protruding belly and enlarged breasts, I had ignored them despite being at least four months from conception.

After the miscarriage my mind blocked out the specifics. It took me years to acknowledge what had happened, to repent of it, and mourn. It was not until I was finishing at the university that I finally summoned the courage to talk about the loss of my baby.

I had named her privately. And as I wondered about her life and what she would have been like had she lived, I called her by that name. For she had been mine, and mine alone for so very long.

"Baby girl, you were loved but not wanted," I said to her. "And all these years later, you are still loved."

14

A Family Secret

Secrets are like skeletons hanging in a closet waiting to be opened and exposed. Whoever thought it would be possible to keep them hidden? Surely, it was the great Deceiver.

The longer that secret thoughts and furtive deeds remain buried, the easier it is to believe they will never be discovered. Yet they are rarely locked away for good. No matter the lengths to which we go to conceal them, their whereabouts are eventually revealed.

My mother was present at the genesis of a deep secret well before my conception. It was kept under wraps until it spread in whispers throughout the family like a smoldering fire emitting a slowly rising cloud of ash.

In my eyes my father had always been a giant. Maybe that was because my mother worked so hard to depict him as evil, but I refused to believe it. Or maybe it was due to the trusting love of a daughter for whom her father was the savior when her mother was the enemy. Whatever the reason, my father could do no wrong until my eyes were opened wide enough to see it.

My father had many girlfriends. But because I was allowed to visit him only every other weekend, to me they were strangers. Only occasionally did one of them stay around long enough for me to remember her name. Most of them, being single mothers with children of their own, were easy prey for my father. Given the dysfunctional relationships they had with their own fathers and ex-husbands, my father was the man who paid them some much needed attention. If you had asked them about him, they probably would have said that he was a good man. But nothing could have been further from the truth. For behind him he left a trail of lovers whose hearts he had broken.

The courts had decided that two weekends a month, plus one week in the summer, constituted a sufficient amount of time for a father to build a relationship with his children. As more and more of my classmates' families split up, I learned that this was the visitation norm.

My father had always said that he wanted more time with my sister and me but that my mother wouldn't allow it. From his point of view, and mine at the time, he saw her as the greatest barrier to our having a relationship with him. But in reality he did not realize just how he had become his own worst enemy.

Work and women were the twin idols absorbing his time and attention. The inordinate hours he spent on the job to support his desired lifestyle, added to the number of women with whom he surrounded himself, came at a great cost to us as his children. We always took third place in importance.

As I grew older, I became increasingly aware of his dysfunction. During our weekend visitations, his girlfriend's children were often with him too. Since those children invariably spent more time with him than we did, his closeness to them incurred our resentment.

Although for years I had loved and trusted my father, there nevertheless seemed to be a dark cloud increasingly hovering about us whenever we were together. Deep down I felt that something was off track, and that it was due to more than the deficiency of time I spent in his presence.

As tensions grew between us, and as I became a more rebellious teenager, our fights gradually escalated. When I was about age sixteen, I felt that he no longer held that special place in my life that he once had. My rose-colored glasses shattered as I observed him cheat on one woman after another.

Our first disagreements took place over the plans he failed to keep when he was supposed to be with us, and over his whereabouts when he was not. Then they grew into full-blown arguments about the women he was hurting. As a result, my feelings toward him turned icy cold like the winds of an arctic winter.

* * *

While growing up, I used to hear my uncle often tell about my surprise appearance in the family. He always framed it in terms of my mother having called the house where he and his family were living, to announce my birth by exclaiming, "It's a girl!"

To me, that seemed like a somewhat odd yet endearing story. Later I learned that it was anything but endearing. At the age of nineteen, I finally began to piece together the details about the family secret that everyone had been keeping.

It was after an intense year of battling with my father that, one day, an aunt, who consistently maintained a listening ear and an open heart, released a part of the story to me over the phone. I was explaining to her that I was about to cut my father out of my life, which I had already done with my mother.

Her response to me was forthright: "Cut him a break because he may not be your father."

Until then, I had not known of my mother's affair during her marriage to my father. Nor had I known that my paternity had been in question for nearly two decades. While certain family members knew, none had told me.

So, when I heard my aunt's words, my response to her was epic: "Great! Why didn't anyone tell me before now? It would have saved me a whole lot of frustration, time, and energy."

Actually, I felt some relief. For I said that it would now be much easier for me to cut him off, knowing that he had only been playing daddy with me all along.

But my aunt encouraged me simply to take a break from being around him and speaking with him. That way both of us could calm down and let the tensions dissipate. And because I loved her dearly, that is precisely what I did.

Sometime later, she and I were having a conversation in which I explained to her why my father had hurt me so much.

She comforted me with words I shall never forget.

"Sinners sin, Baby. To expect them to do anything else is crazy."

From that point forward, I prayed for his salvation.

15

Time to Depart

Most babies enter the world surrounded by the love of the people who created them, delivered them, and welcomed them. Unlike those babies, I was a surprise and for the most part a stranger to the larger family into which I was born. I lacked connection to most, other than to the mother who carried me to term. I have wondered if that is why I grew up wanting to be left alone.

My inner circle of trusted people were always welcome in my space, but those I did not know, I did not like. It took time for me to change my opinion of unfamiliar people, even if they were related to me as kinfolk.

As a consequence of the hard-fought battles with my mother, the loss of my own baby, and the conflicts with my father, I remained overwhelmed by all of the distress. I had already been saved once before from my self-destructive instincts, and once again I needed to be saved from retaliating for all of the injustices I had experienced throughout the years. For the sake of my sanity I needed to get away from the fighting, the screaming, and the demonic forces encircling me.

* * *

In high school I worked really hard to keep up my grades for two primary reasons. First, I did not enjoy manual labor. And second, I wanted to live comfortably. Most of my family at the time worked at one of the two major companies in our area, the meat packing plant or the shipyard. And I could not see myself working at either one. So I vowed that I would go to college and become a doctor, a lawyer, and a teacher.

With a grade-point average in the top 5 percent of my high school graduating class, I stood a good chance of fulfilling my dreams. After taking the SAT College Board exams, I received applications from many colleges and universities across the country. Most of them I never filled out. The only ones I considered worth my time were the simple ones requiring easy essays.

My top choice was the University of North Carolina at Chapel Hill. But upon receiving a devastating letter of rejection, I was about to give up hope.

Then one day in March, out of the blue, an application came in the mail from Mary Baldwin College in Virginia. The required information had already been filled in, except for my social security number and signature. The admissions office had even waived the essay requirement and application fee. So I signed it and sent it back without hesitation. Surely this must have been God's intervention, for I had never so much as heard of the place.

By April, I received my acceptance letter, along with scholarship information that included a box to be checked if I wanted to be considered for the ROTC all-female corps of cadets program, which offered additional scholarships.

I checked the box.

* * *

My home life at the time was so tumultuous that I distracted myself as best I could by preparing for school. But then soon after receiving my acceptance letter from Mary Baldwin, my mother and I took to engaging in head-on warfare.

Her goal was to destroy my dream of attending college by flat-out telling me that she would not support me financially. This was the one truthful statement that I readily believed.

And, true to her word, she didn't contribute a single penny toward the degree. In fact, she did everything in her power to hault my financial support, even after I had arrived at the college. As a result, I soon learned the significance of being a dependent on someone else's income tax return.

The scholarship application process required that I enter her financial information since she had claimed me as a dependent when reporting her prior year's taxable income. So when I filed the Free Application for Federal Student Aid, I anticipated a family contribution of 98 percent toward my college expenses. This meant that the government expected my family to support me almost entirely throughout my schooling. Yet my mother refused to sign the document stating that she had claimed me as a dependent on her income taxes. Consequently, I received almost daily phone calls from the college finance office during my first semester.

Whereas I feared I would have to be responsible for the full cost of my college education, God apparently saw fit, where I didn't, to turn the situation in my favor.

For, with my "Expected Family Contribution" reduced to zero, I became eligible for additional financial aid. My mother's refusal to submit her paperwork substantially increased every scholarship I received.

It was explained to me that the basic definition of *favor* is "undeserved merit," which is how I have come to understand the meaning of grace.

In retrospect, as my senior year of high school wound down, my eighteenth birthday fast approached, even as the tormenting fights at home continued to impact my mental state negatively.

So when I went to school on my birthday, I discovered to my delight that I had not missed any days of school. More importantly, because my grades were honorable I was not required to take any final exams.

This was the further confirmation I needed to prepare to depart from my mother's house for good—which is precisely what I did.

Not only so, but having received no financial support from her meant that my future was freed from the tyranny of being her indentured servant.

And that was grace. That was God's favor.

16

Must History Repeat Itself?

After the loss of my baby and the turbulent end to my senior year in high school, I did not want to date. I knew I needed time for my heart, mind, and soul to heal. I was filled with frustration and suppressed anger, which I unleashed in the unhealthiest of ways. Alcohol became my drug of choice because it mellowed my mood swings. I would not let people get close to me lest I be hurt, and in fear that someone might discover my secret about the miscarriage.

Only a few college women in my inner circle were privy to the brutal language that spewed from my mouth, reflecting the old wounds buried deep within my darkened heart. Then, too, the vulgarities spoken by members of the military contributed to the vileness of my tongue.

Given the new and unfamiliar university environment in which I found myself, and not knowing the intentions of the people around me, I built a wall around myself. And to deal with my fears, I regressed into reliving some of the past traumas that offered me a semblance of comfort, if for no other reason than that they were at least familiar.

* * *

After a few months, I came home for a short mid-semester break. And as soon as I entered a local supermarket, there, suddenly, he stood in the aisle, browsing for something.

At that moment I thought of running away. But I realized I could never outrun him or what he represented. He had been a pivotal, and traumatic, part of my past. So when I approached him, we spoke briefly, exchanged phone numbers, and then continued our respective shopping.

Shortly thereafter we spoke by phone. Our initial conversations were light and fluffy with the same sort of getting-to know-you questions we had posed to one another when we first met years prior. Having no knowledge of my pregnancy and subsequent miscarriage, which I did not mention, at age sixteen. So he didn't understand when I said that I had no desire to see him anymore. The wall between us had grown considerably, and I was in self-preservation mode. There were too many challenges for me to navigate, and my safety and security took precedence.

Nevertheless, our phone conversations continued. And as they progressed, they became more intimate. He shared the trauma he had experienced with his former girlfriend whom he had dated after our relationship ended. Hearing how painful and life-altering that had been, I began to open my heart to him again. With a blossoming desire, I felt increasingly captivated, all the while knowing that he was by no means healed from the ordeal.

* * *

Late one night, at the end of an extended conversation, he said the three dreaded words, "I love you!" And, suddenly, I had to decide whether or not to return the sentiment. I did care for him. I wanted only the best for him. And I knew that he needed to know that someone still loved him. So I said, "I love you."

Still, I had my own unresolved trauma to deal with. So together we sought to help one another with our respective issues. In the process, we dug into old wounds that continued to fester, some of which we had inflicted upon each other, until eventually our conversations triggered something I had not experienced with him before—his rage.

So, when he cursed me, I immediately hung up the phone.

It was not as though I had never heard such words or used them myself, but hearing him speak to me like that raised a bright red flag.

Apparently, he felt some remorse because he called my cell phone repeatedly for the next hour. Then a few hours later he called one last time and left a voicemail, apologizing for his hostility.

It was noon the following day that I finally returned his call. I first let him apologize, after which I drew a clear and definitive line in the sand as to how he could speak to me. He agreed to my terms and we moved on with the conversation, turning to a totally different topic.

But the damage had already been done. From that point forward I was vigilant about noticing the red, yellow, and green flags in our relationship. And as we talked each week with greater frequency, seeking to repair broken aspects of our shared past, the flags flew in every direction, just like the legions of flags fluttering in the wind at the United Nations. Yet we were anything but united.

After several months, I gave myself the okay to end the relationship once and for all, and I called him one night to say that we needed to talk about a very serious subject.

As we spoke, I could hear the commotion of voices and music in his background, which made it difficult for us to hear what the other was saying. So I politely asked him to find a quieter spot.

It was then that I heard another female call his name, saying, "I love you." That was the straw that broke the camel's back. Immediately, a difficult conversation became an extremely simple one. "It's over!" I said, and hung up.

When I blocked his number from calling my phone, he surely got the point.

* * *

Now that the relationship at last was over, I began soul-searching, only to discover the mountainous clouds of darkness that still blocked my path forward. I was already working to quit using profanity since I had been told that it was "unladylike." And for the next few years I did quite well at watching my tongue. But viewing pornography crept back into my life as a weekly routine.

So then I decided to turn in a different direction.

I began reading the Bible, which had a transformative effect upon my mind and soul, as well as upon my flesh!

I was struck.

I was struck by what Jesus said in response to the scribes and Pharisees who questioned why he and his disciples didn't engage in the ritual washing of their hands when they ate bread.

He said: *"It is not what goes into the mouth that defiles a person, but it is what comes out of the mouth that defiles"* (Matt 15:11).

His words pierced right through to the marrow of my bones. For here was the clearest reason yet—and from the Bible, no less—for renouncing the profane language that had spewed from my mouth at every turn.

Moreover, during the remainder of my college years, I made significant changes in other respects. And, although I was not without my failures and setbacks, I nevertheless submitted myself wholeheartedly to Christ. I was baptized in water and filled with the Holy Spirit.

As a consequence, my mission in life changed too. Most importantly, I knew that God was right there with me, no matter what else might come my way.

17

Guardian Angels

G od graciously saw to it that angels in the form of surrogate mother figures surrounded me, guarded me, protected me, and, most significantly, loved me when my own mother did not.

When I was a small child, my next-door neighbor, a cousin, became that much needed angel. In as much as I felt useless or worthless, her words filled me with love, joy, and happiness. She had no children of her own but she actively shared her love with all of the children around her. I considered myself to be one of hers.

Nearly every day she called me "pretty little girl," which meant more to me than I could say. Because she so wonderfully affirmed me, the opinions that others held of me didn't matter so much, and I could look in the mirror and see the beauty of God's creation in my own reflection. Even with matted hair, swollen eyes, and puffy cheeks, I could say to myself that I was beautiful. A man calling me pretty could not hold a candle to the light that she shined on my life with her endearing words.

She, like flowers that wilt in the garden, died when I was still young. She never bore any children of her own, but to this day I carry a portion of her most kind and loving spirit within me everywhere I go. I often think of her when I look in the mirror.

Beyond what I received from her, she gave me the power to speak life into the hearts of other children.

* * *

When I was seven or eight, another angel "aunt" entered my life through my mother's second marriage. Although it took some years to realize the extent of her importance, I relished each time we met. She was a peculiar woman. She had two sons but always wished for a daughter. Since she didn't have a little girl of her own, she lavished gifts on her nieces and goddaughter. I, too, was a glad recipient of her love and generosity. She bought us dresses, shoes, hats, purses, and sometimes gloves and lace socks to go with our outfits.

I learned so much from her. She believed in cleaning her house every day. Contrary to the house I grew up in where Saturday mornings were designated for cleaning. It was Pattie Labelle's voice blasting through the walls that beckoned us to get out the mop and broom. Every morning before the sun rose, she mopped her own bathrooms, washed a load of laundry, and swept the floors. I had never stayed with a person who took so much pride in a clean house. I gave her the nickname "Aunt Suzy" for "Suzy Homemaker" because she had homemaking skills in excess, in addition to employment outside her house.

When I left home on the night of my eighteenth birthday, I moved in with her until it was time for me to leave for college. She and her sister purchased most of my dorm supplies. They took me to Walmart to choose whatever I wanted. Aunt Suzy insisted that I have a set of luggage when I went off to college. Until then, an old backpack or shopping bag served me well.

She was a wise woman who offered me her wisdom about men, dating, finances, family, and so much more. She taught me that meals were to consist of two meats, two vegetables, and at least one variety of bread on the table every night when feeding a family full of men. We loved the same movies, watching them over and over again into the wee hours of the morning. For a number of weeks before my departure to the university, we engaged in late night talks about life and love. Then we watched yet another movie until we fell asleep.

* * *

My college's tradition was for the father to place the class ring on his daughter's hand as a symbol of her new life beginning upon graduation. In anticipation of receiving my ring from my dad during my junior year, I thought of calling Aunt Suzy to go shopping with me to purchase a gown to wear to the ball. I had decided on the color but didn't yet have a design. I knew that Aunt Suzy would love to have the opportunity to help me get ready for the occasion. But before I could invite her to accompany me on the shopping spree, as I was walking down the street one day, I received a phone call that turned my world upside down.

Aunt Suzy had suffered a massive stroke that morning and was not expected to live. I felt as if suddenly I had been hit by a Mack truck. Sadly, she died later that night.

I learned a life-changing lesson from that ordeal, which is to tell the ones you love that you love them while there is still a chance to do so. Tomorrow is not promised to any of us.

Losing Aunt Suzy that year made finishing college quite hard, yet I persevered. Thanks to the love of another angel who helped me work through my loss, I kept my focus and completed my schooling.

* * *

Because I came from a large, extended, and close-knit family, another of my kindred aunts offered her support and became my spiritual guide for many years. It wasn't until I was a full-fledged adult living on my own that I recognized her importance for my journey in the faith. She prayed for me, and over me, and interceded on my behalf when I couldn't pray for myself.

She and I also shared some experiences in ministry, but mostly we shared love, laughter, and good food. Her laughter is what I mostly remember when I think of her. The fact that she was never afraid to laugh at herself made it easier for me to accept my own flaws. She often reminded me that she was not perfect. Her humble example as a wife and mother impacted the way I viewed myself as a single person and as a wife and mother in the future. Lighthearted and full of joy, she was very serious about her relationship with Christ.

We spent many holidays together enjoying family and creating memories. She eventually called me her adopted daughter. And when we discovered that she had cancer, I gave her as much of my devotion as if she were my own mother.

* * *

It was a Sunday in June, Father's Day to be exact, that I stopped by her house after church, having noticed that she was absent from the service. When I had walked into the sanctuary that afternoon, she was nowhere to be seen. After the pastor released us from the service, I drove to her house to find her lying on the bed and talking to one of her daughters. She told me of her pain and other symptoms she was experiencing. She then invited me to her bedside to feel her stomach where an enormous mass had begun to protrude. After rubbing it for a few seconds, I thought to myself that, even though she was older than fifty, miracles do happen. So I asked her what seemed like a silly but honest question: "Are you pregnant?" She laughed and said that of course she was not.

When my uncle came home, we decided as a family that she needed to go to the emergency room to be evaluated. They admitted her for some tests that night, and a few days later called the family in for a very difficult conversation. In a room where her father, her husband, her siblings, and her children all gathered, they gave us the devastating news that she had stage-five liver cancer, and that there was nothing else they could do since it was too late for treatment.

After hearing the solemn news, my cousin and I stepped out of the room into the hallway to weep. The doctor had informed us that she likely had another six weeks to live. Whether or not he intended his words as prophesy, it would be exactly six weeks to the day that she left this earthly realm and entered her eternal rest.

The night following her diagnosis, it was my opportunity to stay at the hospital with her. She and I had a long private conversation about her wishes for the remainder of her time. She said she did not ever want to be on life support, so she asked the doctor to add a "Do Not Resuscitate" order to her file. That decision, however, seemed drastic to her children. So we encouraged her to change it instead to a "Do Not Intubate."

As just the two of us sat there in the room together, I asked her whether she accepted the doctor's conclusion or if she preferred to obtain a second opinion. She said that she believed she still had work to do. I affirmed her by saying that I would fight alongside her so long as she wished to keep on fighting. And when she said stop, then we would stop.

The next day I got on the phone and my computer and searched around the country for liver specialists who could offer another opinion. A few days later, after many phone calls, we finally obtained an appointment at The Johns Hopkins University School of Medicine. We then made a road trip to Maryland, where we stayed with her older sister and family, which was the first of many stays I eventually had with them.

Not only was it my first visit there, but it was also the first time I truly understood the meaning of a supportive family that not only enjoyed being together but helped and supported one another through trials and hardships.

My aunt received whatever she desired to eat and drink. Yet because the doctors gave us the same prognosis, saying that the cancer had already destroyed so much of her healthy tissue, a few days later we headed back home to Virginia.

* * *

All of this played out during the week that school ended for me and as I was preparing for my first international teaching position in

Khartoum, Sudan. Day by day, I went about prepping at my house and then driving over to her home to help with her care.

Weeks later, the doctors decided it was time for her to receive hospice care instead of shuffling back and forth for appointments. The hospice personnel graciously arranged her surroundings to accommodate her limited mobility and provided pain management to keep her comfortable.

Before the date that I was to leave the country, I had planned a weekend trip to the mountains with a family that attended my church. I cleared my plan with my aunt who encouraged me to go ahead and have a great time.

I needed that weekend more than I realized. I had spent five straight weeks watching a once vibrant woman of God dwindling down to barely being able to walk, her flesh having thinned to the bones from her loss of appetite. In the mountains among the awesomeness of the magnificent creation I was able to relax and commune with God. The trees, the wind, and the fresh air breathed new life into me.

I returned home renewed and ready to tackle the challenges that lay ahead. In five days I was set to fly out for Sudan.

But two days after returning from the mountains, I received the phone call saying that my aunt had breathed her last during the night.

Once again, an angel whom God had sent to cover me with love and grace had been called home. The pain from mourning her loss seemed unbearable. I wondered if I should ever be able to be close to anyone again. Surely, I could live without the grief, but I could not imagine being bereft of the presence of an angel.

Even so, I took with me the joy, peace, laughter, and beautiful memories of those people who throughout the years had surrounded, guarded, and protected me.

I pressed forward in prayer, taking my cares, troubles, and burdens to God as the source of my strength, so that I could endure, encourage, inspire, and teach.

Perhaps I might even become an angel myself for somebody in need of the same love and grace that had covered my life.

18

God's Given Gifts

My teaching career began in an unconventional manner. While I was not employed as an educator until the age of twenty-one, the cultivation of my gifts as a teacher had begun by the time I turned eight.

As I have said, when I was in elementary school I had the reputation of sometimes terrorizing my teachers, generally because I was bored from not being sufficiently challenged by the content. One principal had the bright idea of not suspending me, but instead, of sending me to a special needs classroom for students who were high school age, semi-mobile, or in wheelchairs.

One student in particular—quiet, quick, and physically strong—was an immediate inspiration. In our first interaction she grabbed my arm and pulled me to the table, inviting me to complete a simple wooden puzzle with her. When we finished, she stood up and retrieved another puzzle from the shelf so that together we could match the pieces. Before I left that day she hugged me tightly, which was the moment my heart opened to children with special needs.

My next "teaching" experience involved my younger brother who was ten years younger than I. His informal education began when I read him Dr. Seuss books each night. By the age of eight months he knew which ones I should read repeatedly as his favorites. By his first birthday I had memorized multiple books from the series for early readers, from which I taught him the letters of the alphabet when I noticed he was tracking them on the printed page. Soon his learning blossomed into reading and writing his own letters and numbers. By the time he was age three he was reading simple patterned books independently of me. I later tutored him in basic math skills that he had not yet acquired by age four. He grew to love math so much that eventually he studied it in college, graduating with a bachelor of science degree in mathematics from Virginia State University.

* * *

During my time at college, the professor who taught the Biology of Women course asked us a profound question, one that altogether shifted my life goal and career path. Her question was this: "If you had to do the same thing every day for the rest of your life, and never get paid for it, what would you do?"

That question unsettled all of my previous thoughts about career choices and required a level of self-analysis unfamiliar to me, more so than the many times I had been asked, "What do you want to be when you grow up?" My professor had awakened me to consider the gifts that God had given me.

My answer to her question, which took me but a few seconds to conclude, was simple: work with children.

The next semester I changed my major from English to psychology, which culminated in my receiving a bachelor of science in psychology with an emphasis in child development. I went on from there to obtain a master's degree in early childhood education from Cambridge College.

* * *

In 2006, as I launched my formal teaching career, which has been my life's calling ever since. I became the general education teacher in a second-grade inclusion class, consisting of 97 percent black and brown students, eighteen out of twenty-four of whom were boys.

After only a few short days, I realized just how much that fatherlessness impacts and plagues our youth. Only two of the students in the class lived in a household with both parents present. The more I probed, which took little effort since eight-year-olds love to tell their story, the more I learned that the preschool-to-prison pipeline is real. In that Title-I school where I taught, more than 75 percent of the students' household incomes were below the poverty line. One after another, they matter-of-factly expressed that their fathers were either in jail, had just gotten out of jail, or were about to go to court. Almost all of their families were to some degree involved with the judicial system.

Due to the normalization of the preschool-to-prison pipeline, none of these children had any idea that this should not have been so. My heart broke especially for the boys whose primary male exemplars were negative role models. So I did all that I could to provide them with direct experiences of successful Black men. On a fairly regular basis I called my male friends and asked them to come and speak to the class. They read the children stories and talked with them about the stories' characters and the importance of personal choices while seated with the children on the carpet. They spent playtime with them outdoors. And after each visit I observed changes in the children's behaviors. The boys were more willing to listen attentively without the threat of imposed consequences, thereby feeling empowered to perform well in their studies. I realized first-hand just how huge an impact adults have on student behavior and achievement, underscoring the critical importance of positive family influences.

* * *

I continued teaching the second grade for another six years and then shifted direction and taught kindergarten. On my first day in the kindergarten classroom, I had twenty-five students who were four and five years of age. This, too, was a Title-I school, required by law to have a maximum of seventeen students per class. But it was not so. Each of the four teachers on our team was initially assigned twenty-four or twenty-five students. By the time the administration made adjustments to the class size, each teacher was left with twenty-one or twenty-two students to educate.

It has been scientifically proven that smaller class sizes have a positive correlation to increased student academic achievement. Yet we as professional educators consistently make decisions to ensure that minority students do not benefit from fewer class members. Teachers are required to complete inordinate amounts of paperwork, to give more time to at-risk students with greater emotional needs, and all the while teach with limited resources and training. These factors, among others, cause many of the best teachers to quit the profession or move into non-teaching roles where they are better compensated.

* * *

After teaching kindergarten for that one year, I made the decision to change direction altogether. I had been praying for God to show me how best to use my gifts and talents in more rewarding work, and, if possible, to do so in another country. While I waited, I served the community in which I lived. But as I became increasingly frustrated, I prayed and asked again, "Can I go now?" God's answer, however, seemed to take an eternity.

In 2009, while still waiting, I found a way to get out of debt, which I managed to accomplish in 2011, when I asked again, "Father, can I go now?"

"Wait" was the answer.

So that year I learned to engage in fasting and to study God's word in the Bible. Then in 2012 I asked to go again, but God responded, "Not yet, daughter." So that same year I bought my first house. And then, in 2014, I asked once more.

And God said, "Get prepared. Now you can go."

I had spent the 2013–2014 school year with my kindergarten babies, loving on them as hard as I could, because I knew this would be the last time I'd see them. One of the marks of a great teacher is that, year after year, former students return to visit and check on their teacher. Likewise the teacher checks on them. But it would not be so for these children since I was headed to another tribe, another kindred, and another nation.

※ ※ ※

Having packed my luggage, in the wee hours of the morning I headed to the airport with my immediate family joining to see me off. I had never traveled to or through any country on the continent of Africa. The closest I had come to the motherland was visiting the island of Cyprus in the Mediterranean Sea. But now my destination was Khartoum in the Sudan.

The journey was not only about getting away from what was familiar to me, but about growing closer to God. I had left home without expectations about the new mission upon which I was embarking, but I knew deep down from within that my Lord Jesus was going before me, and that I was called to follow him. I was fully confident that my path had been prepared and that I would not beg for bread. God had proven himself faithful to me time and again. My church family had prayed for me. My biological family had prayed over me as well, even though their prayers were mixed with worries. As we said our goodbyes, tears were shed and I walked to the escalator, being careful not to look back.

The journey included two long layovers, one at JFK Airport in New York City, and the other in Doha, Qatar. Upon landing safely at the Khartoum International Airport, I was glad to be done with flying for a while. But something strange and unexpected happened just before we departed from the cabin.

One of the flight attendants began opening spray cans as an announcement played over the intercom, saying it was necessary to spray for mosquitoes before opening the doors. Even though by then it was too late for me to change course since I had already landed at my destination, for the first time I seriously questioned my decision.

Nevertheless, I stepped out of the plane as a blast of stiff hot air from the midnight sun signaled that my adventure had begun.

I was met at the terminal gate by someone holding a sign with my name on it, which was also to be the case when I later traveled to teach in China and then Dubai. As amazing as it was to see my name written upon such welcome signs, I couldn't help but think of the day when my name was written in the Lamb's book of life. For as I traveled the globe, each destination taught me all the more about God's loving kindness.

My church family welcomed me in China. I gained Russian, Ghanaian, South African, and Brazilian brothers and sisters in Christ. We worshipped, praised, prayed, and traveled together like a family. My Sunday mornings bespoke of the many tribes and nations that dwell together in heaven. It was a beautiful sight to see brothers and sisters dwelling in unity and worshipping God as one body. When I reached Dubai, my family expanded even more, to include Nigerians, Kenyans, and Filipinos.

In each of these countries God gave me the gifts with which to teach God's word to the children in churches and homes, in order to advance God's kingdom on earth. In Dubai, I had the opportunity to teach women as well, welcoming them into my circle of friends, from which they in turn went out to teach and preach the gospel.

Jesus said, "Suffer the little children unto me."

Just so, it was in his steps, and with his help, that I sought to follow his commandment, to go and make disciples of all nations. For it is he who is as bright as the sun to our eyes, to show us the way.

Afterword

My life and my story are an amazing testament to the goodness of God. The grace that God offers to all of us is what made me the woman I am today. Although I have known hatred, sorrow, and pain, I have also known love, hope, and joy. I pray that my story has helped you to see that, no matter how many challenges, disappointments, or setbacks you have faced, your life can change for the better. I have shared with you some of the most important lessons that I have learned thus far, and I hope they will be of help to you in your journey through life. Here are a few of those lessons:

Forgiveness is for setting you free. Yet, when your anger and resentment hold another person in a state of unforgiveness, you both remain imprisoned. Forgiveness is a choice, a hard one sometimes, but always a necessary one. We forgive because we have been forgiven.

Hatred is a demonic spirit that, like an all-consuming fire, destroys from the inside out. When hatred is stored in the heart, waiting to be directed toward some person in your life, it invariably will seep out and do its work of destruction. There is only one way to overcome it, and that is by love. For it is love that conquers hate. Choose therefore to love, even when it is immensely difficult.

Knowing who you are, and *whose* you, enables you to walk in the way of your divine calling, to bless the world with your presence and gifts and talents. Know that the words you speak of yourself, to others and of others, will bring life or death. Words are seeds planted in the heart to take root, sprout, and blossom, for good or ill. So, be mindful of the words and thoughts you allow to take root in you. Speak life to yourself, and speak life to others.

Self-control is the key to achieving what is best for you. If you master it, then sin will not master you. When you are facing trials and temptations, exercising self-control protects your heart against those momentary desires of the flesh that can entrap your mind, body, and will, causing you to sin and become less than you are worth. So, aim for self-control in all that you do.

Whatever you may be praying for, believe with all your heart that you will receive it, if it is God's will.

I prayed for healing, and God delivered it to me. I pray that God will do the same for you.

www.ingramcontent.com/pod-product-compliance
Lightning Source LLC
LaVergne TN
LVHW021611080426
835510LV00019B/2519